THE AWESOME MERCY OF GOD

THE AWESOME MERCY OF GOD

John H. Hampsch, C.M.F.

PUBLISHED BY ST. ANTHONY MESSENGER PRESS
CINCINNATI, OHIO

Scripture passages have been taken from *New Revised Standard Version Bible*, copyright ©1989 by the Division of Christian Education of the National Council of the Churches of Christ in the U.S.A., and used by permission. All rights reserved.

Catechism quotations are taken from *Catechism of the Catholic Church* (CCC), second edition (Washington: United States Catholic Conference, 1997).

Cover design by Steve Eames
Book design by Phillips Robinette, O.F.M.

LIBRARY OF CONGRESS CATALOGING-IN-PUBLICATION DATA

Hampsch, John H.
  The awesome mercy of God / John H. Hampsch.
    p. cm.
  ISBN 0-86716-761-0 (pbk. : alk. paper)
  1. God—Mercy. 2. Christian life—Catholic authors.   I. Title.
  BT153.M4H36 2006
  231'.6—dc22

                             2005027789

ISBN-13 978-0-86716-761-0
ISBN-10 0-86716-761-0

Published by Servant Books, an imprint of St. Anthony Messenger Press.
28 W. Liberty St.
Cincinnati, OH 45202
www.AmericanCatholic.org

Printed in the United States of America.

Printed on acid-free paper.

06 07 08 09 10 5 4 3 2 1

I stand in awe, O Lord, of your work....
In our own time...remember mercy.
—Habakkuk 3:2

TABLE OF CONTENTS

PREFACE

While driving through a bustling business district, my attention was captured by a prominent sign that read, "Working at the Same Spot for 10 Years." I realized that it was a pun, intended or otherwise, when I saw that the business was a dry-cleaning establishment!

My subdued chuckle segued into an afterthought as I analogized the words with the situation of many distraught souls who seek my help in spiritual direction. Slogging through life under the psychological burden of guilt feelings—and often real moral guilt too—they've been "working at the same spot" to no avail for so long that it has sometimes resulted in serious emotional and also physical (psychosomatic) disorders. Their hearts feel, in the graphic words of my farmer uncle, "as heavy as a bucket of hog livers." Their psyches are so paralyzed by guilt that they cannot assimilate the words of Jesus: "Do not let your hearts be troubled" (John 14:1, 27).

Of all twenty-seven emotions, guilt is probably the most corrosive to our physical and emotional integrity.

Sincere souls beset by such anguish usually have at least a faint awareness that God has the answer, and their pleadings reflect those of David: "Let your steadfast love become my comfort according to your promise.... Let your mercy come to me" (Psalm 119:76–77).

Jesus stated emphatically, "Very truly, I tell you, everyone who commits sin is a slave to sin," then went on to announce the liberating effect of allowing him to lift that burden by his proffered mercy: "If the Son makes you free, you will be free indeed" (John 8:34, 36).

Guilt is a moot issue for those who, by their vibrant faith and *boundless trust in the Lord*, are deeply convinced of the abundance and availability of God's gracious mercy. They are aware of the Lord's passionate desire to deliver them from such bondage—without their having to "work at the same spot" in an extended effort. Souls who have been Spirit-nurtured in trust do not doubt God's power and willingness to wipe away their sin: "Blot out all my iniquities. Create in me a clean heart, O God" (Psalm 51:9–10).

Saint Faustina, the heaven-chosen and ardent campaigner for the Divine Mercy devotion, bannered an invitation to the heart of God at the direction of Jesus himself. It consisted of a paraphrase of Psalm 33:22, a brief but all-encompassing ejaculatory prayer of reliance on our Lord himself: "Jesus, I trust in you."

The devotion to the Divine Mercy takes on a special meaning in our tumultuous age of unspeakable evils, in which moral and physical evils are often interfused—as in the case, for instance, of venereal disease pandemics. And this devotion would seem to carry even eschatological overtones because of the special commission that Jesus assigned to Saint Faustina, as recorded in her diary, to prepare the world for his final coming. That truly gives pause for serious thought. And it also provided for me the motivational capstone for authoring this book, to hopefully further a wider interest in such a crucial spiritual concern.

With Pope John Paul II's canonization of Sister Faustina as the first saint of this millennium and his simultaneous establishment of the Feast of Divine Mercy (the Sunday after Easter), this devotion has gained phenomenal prestige in Catholic circles. I ask the reader to join me in prayer, pleading that this little treatise will extend this devotion to all people everywhere, enticing them to enjoy the freedom, joy and peace that God's loving mercy affords. Ultimately, may it all redound solely to God's glory.

One

A HEAVEN-DESIGNED JIGSAW PUZZLE

I f you are interested in a fascinating experiment, just try this: Take a fresh sponge—not a plastic sponge but a regular ocean sponge, which is actually a living entity, like coral—and cut it into hundreds of pieces. Then scatter all the pieces in a tank of water and leave them untouched overnight. The next morning you will find that the pieces have reassembled themselves into the exact shape of the original intact sponge—like a spontaneously reassembled jigsaw puzzle.

No biologist or other scientist has ever found a satisfactory explanation for this remarkable phenomenon, which is called "reintegrative restoration." It seems to manifest itself in numerous other life forms inhabiting this marvel-spangled Earth. An amputated lizard's tail restores itself to its exact former dimensions, a lava field from a volcanic eruption is eventually reforested, a worm cut in half survives as twin worms, and many nearly extinct species of animals and birds become extant again, overcoming apparently insuperable obstacles. It seems that Divine Providence has introjected into the flora and fauna of our planet a drive for survival that yields an inbuilt dynamic of restoration.

In this great design of restoration in nature, the Creator hasn't forgotten his favorite made-to-the-image-of-God creatures—namely, humans. At the time of the Parousia— the expected second coming of Christ to Earth— humankind's ultimate physical restoration from death will occur (see John 5:29; 11:24). The Apostles' Creed refers to it as "the resurrection of the body." After that event those still living (who will never experience death, as Paul declares in 1 Corinthians 15:51–52) will enjoy a marvelous "rapture" (1 Thessalonians 4:17) and will find themselves restored to a new and instantaneously "spiritualized" body. But between now and that end-time series of momentous events, the "reintegrative restoration" of Homo sapiens is to be found primarily in the *spiritual* dimension of human existence.

WASHED CLEAN

This spiritual restoring is primarily the remarkable cleansing of the human soul from the contamination of acts of evil called sins. The cause of this spiritual (and secondarily physical) restoration is the tender, loving mercy of God, through the resurrected Savior, Jesus Christ, who is "the first fruits of those who have died" (1 Corinthians 15:20) and the prototype of all end-time life-restored humans. The "trigger" that releases this ever-repeatable spiritual restoration in this present life is any and every act of sincere repentance on the part of the "restoree," the

sinner. Amazingly, the very God he has offended rein-
states the sinner to full spiritual integrity.

Unlike the inbuilt "reintegrative restoration" found in
vegetative and animal life, from sponges to lizards,
human restoration is grace-laden, and it involves primarily the exercise of one of the Creator's attributes: his
goodness made relational by his infinite love.
Furthermore, it engages us human creatures in a form of
extremely personal interactivity with our Creator, which
is far beyond the restorative dynamic that works to resta-
bilize the biosphere's ecological balance and even beyond
the "cosmic convalescence" of exploded galaxies.

Some pundit has attempted to poeticize the meaning of
spiritual restoration with the platitude "Christianity
begins where religion leaves off, at the Resurrection." That
can be better understood in the context of John's words
about the Resurrection: "new life," derived from Jesus,
"the faithful witness, the firstborn of the dead,...who
loves us and freed us from our sins" (Revelation 1:5).

The scintillating mind of the great Saint Augustine
explored this wondrous restoration of the human soul as
a spiritual interactivity between the person and our
loving, merciful Lord. He wrote in his *Commentary on the
Gospel of Saint John*:

> Whoever confesses his sins...is already working with
> God. God indicts your sins; if you also indict them, you
> are joined with God. Man and sinner are, so to speak, two
> realities: when you hear "man"—this is what God has
> made; when you hear "sinner"—this is what man himself
> has made. Destroy what you have made, so that God may
> save what he has made.... When you begin to abhor what

you have made, it is then that your good works are beginning, since you are accusing yourself of your evil works.
The beginning of good works is the confession of evil works
(italics mine).[1]

To say that "the beginning of good works is the repentance for evil works" is another way of saying that conversion starts with justification—that is, with spiritual
restoration from a state of sinfulness. But justification, a
relative term, needs completion itself in the endless striv-
ing for sanctification—that is, growth in holiness, grace
and virtue—toward becoming "perfect, therefore, as your
heavenly Father is perfect" (Matthew 5:48).

To transform a scraggly plot into a garden initially
requires weeding and seeding, then mending and tend-
ing. To continue to cultivate and enjoy that garden, one
must commit to an endless process of attaining and
maintaining its beauty. Between the seed stage and the
flower stage of the soul, it is "God who gives the growth"
(1 Corinthians 3:7). Our cooperative reciprocation is to
"grow in the grace and knowledge of our Lord and Savior
Jesus Christ" (2 Peter 3:18). Thus God's mercy nudges us
to move beyond justification through repentance into the
full bloom of sanctity.

The *Catechism of the Catholic Church* (1989) elucidates
this process by showing that a conversion of soul is initiated by repentance, which in turn effects justification. The
soul responds to Jesus' earliest proclamation in his mission, "Repent, for the kingdom of heaven has come near"
(Matthew 4:17), thus accepting forgiveness and righteousness from on high. The Council of Trent stated that "justi-

fication is not only the remission of sins, but also the sanctification and renewal of the interior man."[2]

Thus the process, *initiated by accepting God's mercy* for forgiveness (triggered by repentance), "justifies" the soul, detaching it from sin and sinful habits, and embellishes (sanctifies) it with grace-watered virtues, resulting in a renewal (restoration) of one's spiritual life. The unkempt plot, now weeded and fertilized, blossoms in holiness—a holiness by reason of the vibrant life of grace, the participation in the very life of God absorbed from the divine Gardener himself. Second Peter 1:4 refers to us as "participants of the divine nature." And the life of God is full, "abundant," as John 10:10 says. The flowers don't droop or wilt; they burst forth in a riot of color and beauty. And the Gardener smiles on the God-mirrored soul, for "the Holy God shows himself holy by [our] righteousness" (Isaiah 5:16).

Peter described the process well:

His divine power has given us everything needed for life and godliness, through the knowledge of him who called us by his own glory and goodness. Thus he has given us, through these things, his precious and very great promises, so that through them you may escape from the corruption that is in the world because of lust, and may become participants of the divine nature. For this very reason, you must make every effort to support your faith with goodness, and goodness with knowledge, and knowledge with self-control, and self-control with endurance, and endurance with godliness, and godliness with mutual affection, and mutual affection with love. For if these things are yours and are increasing among you, they keep you from being ineffective and unfruitful in the

knowledge of our Lord Jesus Christ. For anyone who
lacks these things is short-sighted and blind, and is forget-
ful of the cleansing of past sins. (2 Peter 1:3–9)

The option of spiritual restoration is ours. Just as we
choose to sin, we can choose to repent and thus elicit
God's restorative mercy. "Cast away from you all the
transgressions that you have committed against me, and
get yourselves a new heart and a new spirit!" (Ezekiel
18:31).

But it is God who initiates the restoration. The plea
comes from his very heart: "Return to the LORD, your
God, for he is gracious and merciful, slow to anger, and
abounding in steadfast love, and relents from punishing"
(Joel 2:13).

MERCIFUL LOVE

The Chicago Public Library recently declared an
"amnesty day" for borrowers of overdue books. With no
fines and no questions asked, over ten thousand books
were returned, some overdue since 1934!

Every day is "amnesty day" with God. He's more eager
to forgive us our debts than we are eager to be forgiven.
"You, O Lord, are good and forgiving, abounding in
steadfast love to all who call on you" (Psalm 86:5).

Who would not call on him? Who more than a prisoner
enjoys freedom? And who more than a sinner should
enjoy God's forgiveness? Since everyone is a sinner (First
John 1:8 says, "If we say that we have no sin, we deceive
ourselves, and the truth is not in us"!), we can all rejoice
that forgiveness doesn't tax our resources but only our

Savior's. It is "the blood of Jesus," not our own efforts, that "cleanses us from all sin" (verse 7).

At the return of an "overdue" sinner, no questions will be asked; we merely return to God in humble repentance. Any Magdalene can hear the gentle, forgiving voice of Jesus urging her to sin no more. A dying thief can hear the promise of an immediate paradise. The housewife with her peccadilloes of impatience can feel the soothing balm of Christ's tender mercy. The inconsiderate husband can see his selfishness replaced by the selflessness of a strong but kindly Jesus. The child can see his little flaws of disobedience melt in the springtime smile of the lover of little ones. The ear of God is always attuned to hear the sheepish words "I'm sorry" as we "approach the throne of grace" to "receive mercy" (Hebrews 4:16).

We return and God restores. The restoration itself entails a dialogue, not merely a divine monologue. This marvelous process is mentally and spiritually intoxicating to ponder at length, simply because it launches us into the fathomless realm of the infinite love of God. Granted, infinity is something that the human mind is incapable of encompassing. We can begin to apprehend it—that is, perceive it and be aware of it—but we can't comprehend it. God's love is so big that he sent Jesus to suffer and die for murderers, thieves, prostitutes, drug traffickers, adulterers, perverts, drunks, tyrants—and me.

The reason why it's hard for us to appreciate fully God's merciful love is that we can't fathom the depth of that kind of love. It's simply beyond us—beyond our capacity as humans—to love so unconditionally and so universally. God hates sin with a hatred that we can't imagine, but he profoundly loves the person who commits the sin. The world's worst sinner is precious to God, who lovingly desires that he be saved. Paul says in Romans 11:28: "As regards the gospel they are enemies of God,...but as regards election [eligibility for salvation] they are beloved." Thus love and hate comprise a double-edged sword that is sheathed in the truism traditionally attributed to Saint Augustine, "God hates the sin but loves the sinner."

On his part God is yearning with his merciful love to save the sinner who is still eligible to be saved. Such a one is like the starving person who is still able to eat food that is offered to him. We think of the "good thief," known now as Dismas, "the thief who stole heaven" while dying on Calvary. Jesus promised him that he would be in paradise with him that very day, the first Good Friday.

God's mercy extends to all except those who refuse it, as did the "other thief" next to Jesus on the cross—the apparently obdurate one, traditionally known as Gestas. The only "unforgivable" persons are the reprobates who freely refuse God's forgiveness. Some even respond to God's offer of mercy by redoubling rather than reversing their malevolence toward him. The infamous King Ahaz "in the time of his distress...became yet more faithless to the LORD" (2 Chronicles 28:22). And before that the wicked Amaziah refused to listen to God's prophet and so was doomed to destruction (see 25:14–16). Such refusals become irrevocable when a soul enters hell.

Let's take a more discriminating look at the two-edged sword of love and hate. "Love the sinner, hate the sin" has become a veritable shibboleth in moral theology. God loves the mafioso hit man, the drug trafficker, the genocidal tyrant and the holocaust executioner just as much as he loves the saintly contemplative nun wrapped in prayer—in the quantitative sense, that is. He loves both saint and sinner infinitely and, in that measure, equally.

However, his infinite love differs in each person by reason of the amount of grace conferred and also in the quality (or degree) of intimacy that is the expression of his love. Thus God's equally infinite love for both saint and sinner is differently mirrored in each person, according to the varying degrees of each person's acquiescence to God's will. When thus differentiated we can understand how "his mercy is for those who fear [reverence] him" (Luke 1:50).

The nineteenth-century preacher of fame Henry Ward Beecher wrote: "There is dew in one flower and not another, because one opens its cup and takes it in, while the other closes itself.... God rains his goodness and mercy as widespread as the dew, and if we lack them, it is because we will not open our hearts to receive them."[3]

A TRUE LOOK AT GOD

In a kindergarten art session the teacher asked a little girl what she was drawing. She answered that it was a picture of God. The teacher gently reminded the child that no one knows what God looks like. The moppet replied, "They will when I finish!"

As Voltaire opined, God has made us to his image, but we tend to make him into ours.[4] We tend to impose our limitations on our concept of God. We expect him to love as little as we do, to forgive only what we would forgive.

Even great minds like that of Desiderius Erasmus struggled against that tendency to anthropomorphize God. In his lucid prose C.S. Lewis wrote, in *The Problem of Pain*, that "we regard God as an airman regards his parachute; it's there for emergencies, but he hopes he'll never have to use it."[5]

My challenge in writing this book is to loft the reader's perception of God above such pedestrian and myopic views of our ineffably tender, loving, merciful Father. I hope to impress readers with the fact that for God, unlike us humans, offering forgiveness isn't an occasional act; it's a permanent attitude, a divine and eternal prerogative.

Scripture overflows with images expressing how God erases our sin: "I have swept away your transgressions like a cloud, and your sins like mist" (Isaiah 44:22). "He will tread our iniquities under foot" (Micah 7:19). "The blood of Jesus…cleanses us from all sin" (1 John 1:7). "I will forgive their iniquity, and remember their sin no more" (Jeremiah 31:34).

The prolixity of Scripture on the topic of God's mercy is amazing; it would be difficult to find any other topic treated so extensively in God's Word. That fact, along with Pope John Paul II's encyclical on the mercy of God, *Dives in Misericordia*, provides the best possible support for the authenticity of the relatively modern devotion to the mercy of God, promoted by the unprecedented impetus of Jesus' revelations to Saint Faustina.

Jesus himself strives, by reliable revelation, public and private, to correct our absurdly distorted and harshly cropped view of his great attribute of Divine Mercy and compassion, which "is over all that he has made" (Psalm 145:9). His words to Sister Faustina are indicative of the depths of this attribute: "My mercy is so great that no mind, be it of man or of angel, will be able to fathom it throughout all eternity."[6] Even the far-beyond-human intellects of the highest of the nine choirs of angels, the seraphim and cherubim, with their profound insights that will grow ever deeper for all the endless ages of eternity, will never be able to comprehend the greatness of God's attribute of Divine Mercy! Yet God entices us to try, at least, to fathom the fathomless. What better way to grow in knowing him and his love?

Before we "launch out into the deep," we must assist our advancement by "weighing anchor." It is appropriate for this treatise about God's mercy to begin with a strong emphasis on the premiere purpose of God's mercy— admittedly its negative aspect—namely, the disencumbering of the soul from its anchor, its sin-burden. In subsequent parts of the book, we move on to the more "positive" aspects of his mercy, such as the bestowal of graces, intercessory mercy by the "works of mercy," spiritual gifts, health, food, sustenance, resources and more. "Your heavenly Father knows that you need all these things" (Matthew 6:32).

The overview of both the negative and positive aspects is summarized in the Epistle to the Hebrews, which discloses that the Lord enables us to "receive mercy and find grace" (Hebrews 4:16). That is, he erases the blemishes of sin (negative) and enriches our lives with myriad helps (positive).

I venture to suggest that the multiple dimensions of this breathtaking prerogative of the Almighty deserves no less a name than the title of this book, *The Awesome Mercy of God*.

TWO

WHERE DO THE SINS GO?

Here's a brainteaser for you. If a traveler on Earth were to travel east, he could do so endlessly without changing directions. The same would be true if he traveled west. But it would not be true if he chose to travel endlessly north or south from any place on Earth. Any northbound traveler would inevitably reach and cross the North Pole, finding himself then headed south. Likewise a southbound traveler would ultimately cross the South Pole and, continuing, would find himself northbound. Even a northeast-bound traveler would find himself headed southeast eventually, and choosing a northwest trajectory would have him headed southwest. Why?

These anomalies are true because Earth's axis is a north-south one. If the rotational axis were to become unstable and "horizontalized," so as to pierce the equator, the eastbound traveler would eventually travel west. We would have an East Pole and a West Pole, and a person could head north or south endlessly.

Earth's axis is quite stable, but its Creator, "with whom there is no variation" (James 1:17), is even more stable: "I the LORD do not change" (Malachi 3:6). It is the unchanging word of this unchanging God that purposely uses the west-to-east analogy—not a north-to-south one—in describing his irreversible disposal of sin: "As far as the east is from the west, so far he removes our transgressions from us" (Psalm 103:12).

But just how far is the east from the west? As explained above, it must be "infinitely distant." That is, sins "sent off" in an easterly direction will never be reversed to a westerly direction. *So forgiven sins must be gone forever, irretrievably!* If you stop and mull over that amazing truth for a moment, you will never suffer from guilt feelings (also known as a "guilt complex") about any past sins already sincerely confessed!

If you feel that you are on a perpetual "guilt trip," even after sincerely repenting of past sins, you need to know that the merciful Lord didn't send you down that road. You probably set up your own miserable itinerary (a north-south journey, perhaps?). The devil planned your send-off with a farewell jeer: *Mal voyage!*

Symbols of Mercy

A Bible school teacher strove to impress upon the youngsters in her class the wonders of God's forgiveness of our sins. To that end she quoted the passage from Isaiah 38:17: "You have cast all my sins behind your back."

But one perspicacious child challenged the teacher about this. "Even if my sins were put behind God's back," the little girl said, "he could still see them if he turned around."

The clever teacher simply took a black marker and put a number of X's on a sheet of paper. She explained that these marks represented the little girl's sins. She then called a boy forward and taped the marked paper on his back. She asked the boy to turn around and look at the black marks on the paper. The other pupils laughed as they realized that, no matter which way the lad turned, the symbolic sins were always behind him and out of his sight! From that day the profound truth of that passage from Isaiah resides in each of these children's memories.

Encouraged by her successful pedagogical tactic, the next day the teacher went on to demonstrate another scriptural passage about God's merciful love. She made some ugly scrawls on the blackboard and told the youngsters that the scrawls represented the sins on one person's soul. Then came her simple "magic." Explaining that "this sinner decided to repent," she erased every bit of every mark. Then she turned to the youngsters and asked, "Where did the sins go? Did they go into the next room? Or out onto the playground? Or under my desk?"

To every question the kids screamed: "No!" They were forced to conclude that the sins went nowhere; they just disappeared. They no longer existed—anywhere. When one child exclaimed that they were "blotted out," the teacher took her cue and tied in the previous day's lesson with a quote from Psalm 51:9: "Hide your face from my sins, and blot out all my iniquities." With that she made it possible for her pupils to possess another gem from the treasure trove of God's Word.

It's not just children who wonder where sins go when remitted—which is like wondering what happens to forgotten memories. Many honest adults are unsure about this too. When I received that question recently in an E-mail, I couldn't resist referring facetiously to the man who stayed up all night wondering what happened to the sun after it sank below the horizon. It finally "dawned" on him!

The first European pilgrimage for which I served as chaplain started with a lengthy transatlantic voyage on an ocean liner. One day on the deck, braving a blustering ocean wind, I was chatting with one of the pilgrims when I noticed that she was wearing a costly gold amulet engraved with a pagan symbol. I told her that to wear it was a sin of superstition. More than that, it was an insult to the one true God, because she was giving acknowledgment to a false god.

The woman hadn't realized the seriousness of the matter until I explained it to her. She ripped the amulet from her neck, along with its gold chain, and threw it overboard, watching it sink into utter oblivion.

Because of her ignorance she had no malice, and hence no sin, in this matter. However, she insisted that I give her confessional absolution on the spot for all the sins of her life—right there on the wave-lashed deck, in the midst of an ocean windstorm. She wanted that amulet to represent all the sins of her life as it sank irretrievably to the depths of the ocean floor.

I couldn't resist mentioning the prophet Micah's reference to sin-disposal in the ocean of God's mercy: "You will cast all our sins into the depths of the sea" (Micah 7:19).

From now until the end of the world, no one will ever see that amulet, and no demon will ever be able to point to her sins that are symbolically submerged with it, forever out of sight.

Where do our sins go? As one hymn writer quaintly phrased it, "My sins are now in the sea of God's forgetfulness."

What Sins?

There is a story about a man who repeatedly begged God for forgiveness for a sin that he had committed countless times. As he eagerly listened for the Lord's reply, the Lord finally spoke to him: "You are forgiven, my son."

"But, Lord," the man queried, "how can you forgive this sin so easily, after all those other times I failed in the same way?"

And the Lord asked, "What other times?"

That homey dialogue might well dramatize what Jeremiah wrote in Lamentations 3:22–23: "The steadfast love of the LORD never ceases, his mercies never come to an end; they are new every morning; great is your faithfulness."

In the early centuries of the Christian era, debt certificates and other documents were written on papyrus in a slow-drying ink. Soon after such a certificate was written, it could be completely erased without a trace by wiping it with a wet sponge. That was probably what Paul envisioned as an analogy to divine forgiveness when he wrote in Colossians 2:13–14: "[God] forgave us all our trespasses, erasing the record that stood against us with its legal demands."

I referred in the last chapter to Henry Ward Beecher's analogy between sinners and flowers. The unrepentant thief died next to Jesus as a "closed flower," while the "good" thief was open to receive the "dew" of the saving blood of the God-man dying a few feet away. No one ever asks, concerning the "good" thief, "Where did his stolen loot go?" But no one needs to ask, "Where did his sins go?" He was privileged to be a divine beneficiary of God's mercy at the climactic moment of all of salvation history—a moment that prototyped the perennial choice of acceptance or rejection of God's love. That "bad" day on Calvary thus came to be called "Good" Friday.

There is no crime or sin so terrible that it can dim God's longing to grant forgiveness. And once forgiveness is granted, there is no place for sin to go. Like yesterday or last year, it's gone!

A little-known proclamation from the Council of Trent is certainly encouraging to any thoroughly repentant person: If anyone, because of love for God, sincerely repents of all past sin and also *intends* never to sin again (underscore that word *intends*), then not just all the guilt but even the aftereffect of that guilt is also remitted (see *CCC*, #1472).

The aftereffect of guilt is primarily the temporal (that is, noneternal) purgatorial suffering due to sin. Removal of the accumulated purgatorial debt by God's marvelous mercy occurs only *if* the sinner's trust in God's mercy is absolutely unwavering and intense, with the deepest sincere intention never to sin again. That act of the will (intention) is effective even in the presence of the act of the intellect by which the soul knows it will not remain sinless for the rest of its life.

Sins committed *after* the moment of contrition will have to be dealt with separately. Subsequent purgatorial debt may follow any of thousands of possible ways of failing, such as not embracing generously and lovingly God's will in the timing of one's death or the deathbed agony itself. But God's mercy is available even then, and the efficacy of the Council's proclamation applies also to the dying penitent.

We can with confidence embrace the psalmist's words as our own life song: "Surely goodness and mercy shall follow me all the days of my life, and I shall dwell in the house of the LORD my whole life long" (Psalm 23:6).

Three

GOD'S POOR MEMORY

D uring the first days of his presidency, Calvin Coolidge stayed in a suite at the Willard Hotel in Washington, before he and his family could arrange to move into the White House. Early one morning he awoke to see a burglar removing a wallet and a watch chain from his trouser pockets. Coolidge told the burglar that those items were not that important to him, but he asked him not to take the charm linked to the chain because of the engraving on it.

The robber read the engraving: "Presented to Calvin Coolidge, Speaker of the House, by the Massachusetts General Court."

Dazed by the realization that he was stealing from the newly elected president, he apologized profusely, explaining that he had attempted the thievery because he and his college roommate needed money to pay their hotel bill and the railroad fare back to the college campus. Coolidge opened the wallet and handed him a face-saving "loan" of thirty-two dollars, for which he never expected repayment (though it was later repaid in full). He then advised the lad to avoid alerting the Secret

Service by leaving the hotel suite as unconventionally as he had entered.[1]

This was forgiveness without reprisal, a succinct depiction of Divine Mercy.

The well-known maxim "To err is human; to forgive divine" has been attributed to Abraham Lincoln, for he, like Calvin Coolidge, did not have a vengeful heart. When the Confederate army was finally defeated, Lincoln was asked how he would treat the rebellious Southerners. His magnanimous willingness to forgive was articulated in his unexpected reply: "I will treat them as if they had never been away."[2]

That forgive-and-forget mentality, though rare among humans, reflects God's way of thinking. In fact, forgiveness can be said to depict the mind of God. As Shakespeare put it, "Earthly power doth then show likest God's when mercy seasons justice."[3]

How can it be "divine" to forgive? Human forgiveness partakes of the divine when it encompasses the element of *forgetting*. No, of course God doesn't have a poor memory (that's just the title of this chapter, designed to pique your curiosity). But God does choose not to remember; that is, he refuses to harbor a negative attitude (wrath) toward us sinners when we show sincere repentance.

One second-grader in catechism class described this divine attribute with almost theological perspicacity: "God forgives and forgets, and then he forgets what he has forgiven." Or as a thoughtful quipster phrased it, "When God 'buries the hatchet,' he doesn't mark the gravesite."

Our choice of self-alienation from God—that is, our choice of evil—disappoints him far more than we can ever imagine. But that indescribably deep disappointment on God's part simply "evaporates," as it were, when we truly repent. When we say that God forgives and forgets, we mean that he forgives the sinner and forgets the sin. That's almost a paraphrase of a passage from Hebrews: "I will be merciful toward their iniquities, and I will remember their sins no more" (Hebrews 8:12; see also 10:17).

This "divine forgetting" is mentioned *eight times* in the Bible. God simply refuses to harbor thoughts of our past failings. His love for the precious sinner is incandescent in the Gospels: Jesus shows the father embracing the Prodigal Son on his return home; he saves the adulterous woman from being stoned and promises heaven to the repentant thief dying next to him on Calvary. His loving mercy is the blazing sun that dispels all the darkness, which can then no longer becloud the repentant soul. "Whoever follows me will never walk in darkness but will have the light of life" (John 8:12).

It is insulting to God's goodness to insist on regarding oneself as sin-smeared after the Lord has graciously stooped to cleanse one's soul. That implicit denial of his merciful love can nudge one toward the sin of despair, which violates the virtue of hope. Jesus revealed to one mystic that he is wounded by those who doubt his mercy in this way; such doubt bespeaks unrequited love. Its inner pain, he said, exceeds the physical pain of his Good Friday scourging.

A nonresponse to the offer of God's mercy can take either of two directions: despair or presumption. Both are forms of violation of the virtue of hope, by which we are to reach out to receive God's proffered forgiveness and salvation. The *Catechism of the Catholic Church* spells out this theology very succinctly but clearly:

> By *despair*, man ceases to hope for his personal salvation from God, for help in attaining it or for the forgiveness of his sins. Despair is contrary to God's goodness, to his justice—for the Lord is faithful to his promises—and to his mercy.
>
> There are two kinds of *presumption*. Either man presumes upon his own capacities (hoping to be able to save himself without help from on high), or he presumes upon God's almighty power or his mercy (hoping to obtain his forgiveness without conversion and glory without merit). (*CCC*, #2091–2092)

Souls who really understand and appreciate God's mercy could never fall into either despair or presumption. They would never ask, how much does God forget? They would see that what we forget about God's love is more to the point.

Let's never forget that our God is in the washing business, not the whitewashing business. Our past failings are not varnished; they've vanished. And as he reviews each sin of ours, the Lord doesn't "rub it in"; he rubs it out. "I am He who blots out your transgressions,...and I will not remember your sins" (Isaiah 43:25). "I will cleanse them from all the guilt of their sin" (Jeremiah 33:8).

Paul preached in Antioch, "[T]hrough this man forgiveness of sins is proclaimed to you; by this Jesus everyone who believes is set free from all…sins" (Acts 13:38–39). John reiterated that proclamation of universal sin remission: "[T]he blood of Jesus…cleanses us from all sin" (1 John 1:7). That's *all* sin, *all* guilt. His "forgiving and forgetting" penetrates and cleans every tiny crevice of our being. I've heard the analogy that man is born broken, and the grace of God is the glue for his mending.

This forgiveness is so universal that it includes even seldom-recalled, long-standing and deep-rooted transgressions that fester in the soul. "Do not remember the sins of my youth or my transgressions; according to your steadfast love…Lord!" (Psalm 25:7). "When deeds of iniquity overwhelm us [mind-splintering guilt], you forgive our transgressions" (Psalm 65:3).

Our heavenly Father is so deeply in love with each one of us that he gives us every opportunity to be drawn to him. As Saint Augustine phrased it, "God loves each one of us as if there were only one of us."[4]

To make himself even more accessible and approachable, that we might better receive his mercy, God sets before us his Son as our intercessor (see Romans 8:26–27). Jesus is divine, of course, but still also "one of us."

> For we do not have a high priest who is unable to sympathize with our weaknesses, but we have one who in every respect has been tested as we are, yet without sin. Let us therefore approach the throne of grace with boldness, so that we may receive mercy and find grace. (Hebrews 4:15–16)

That pericope is reminiscent of the Prodigal Son's return to his father's house after a period of dissolute profligacy. "I am no longer worthy to be called your son; treat me like one of your hired hands," he said (Luke 15:19). Instead his father feted him as the guest of honor at a family celebration! The older brother regarded the celebration as wrong, but the father set him right. How often we too underestimate the paternal mercy flowing from "the throne of grace."

If God's restorative mercy seems to be this right, it has to be wrong, right?

Wrong!

FOUR

REPENTANCE: THE SOUL'S "DELETE" FUNCTION

A department store Santa Claus, trying to be kind and complimentary to a youngster, said, "I know everything about you."

He was taken aback by the kid's defensive response: "But, Santa, I've changed!"

Sincere change for the better is essentially an act of the will. There's no mental action more demanding of trust than the act of sincere repentance. We trust the Lord to respond to our protestation that we've really changed, that we've made a "firm purpose of amendment" change as radical as a U-turn, which the early Greek fathers of the church called *metanoia*. In this personalized repentance-forgiveness dialogue, the restoration of the relationship occurs not as the result of mere shame or morbid remorse but rather from a "godly grief [which] produces a repentance that leads to salvation" (2 Corinthians 7:10).

More than four hundred times the Holy Scriptures directly mention God's offer of mercy in response to our repentance. The word depicts mercy for us not only in New Testament parables like that of the lost sheep, the lost coin and the Prodigal Son, but also in real-life stories like the forgiveness of the woman taken in adultery and that of the good thief, who "stole heaven" from his gibbet on Calvary. And of course, underscoring all this is the very real life-and-death story of the torturous atoning passion and death of Jesus himself.

If at any time you are crushed with guilt and need an antidote to despair in your anguish, take a moment to meditate on one of the many pertinent Scriptures alerting us to trust in God's mercy. For example: "Those who trust in him will understand truth, and the faithful will abide with him in love, because grace and mercy are upon his holy ones, and he watches over his elect" (Wisdom 3:9).

If you truly love someone, your love is enriched when your beloved reciprocates that love. A mother hugging her tiny child is thrilled the first time the child displays a reciprocal love response by "hugging back." The Lord revealed to Saint Faustina that nothing gives him greater delight than a soul's loving surrender to his open arms of mercy. The greatest dialogue of love is mercy-love proffered and mercy-love embraced.

The master bard William Shakespeare formulated and immortalized this sublime insight in one of his most frequently quoted passages:

> The quality of mercy is not strain'd,
> It droppeth as the gentle rain from heaven
> Upon the place beneath. It is twice blest—
> It blesseth him that gives, and him that takes.
> Tis mightiest in the mightiest. It becomes

The throned monarch better than his crown....
It is enthroned in the hearts of kings,
It is an attribute to God himself.[1]

Shakespeare's reference to mercy as "an attribute of God" might well incite questions about that very phrase and the theological implications it carries in terms of our respondent spirituality. Theologically considered, there are five so-called primary classical "attributes" or perfections of God: mercy, goodness, generosity, providence and justice. As Saint Thomas Aquinas explains, Divine Mercy, from the human viewpoint, is positioned above all God's works as the premiere attribute.[2] Why? Because God's mercy includes implicitly, and also is manifested through, a number of his "secondary" attributes, such as his kindness, magnanimity, graciousness, clemency, patience and long-suffering.

It is important to note that all of the many attributes of God are really not distinct from each other (or from his very essence) but are differentiated only by human scrutiny and theological analysis. Dissecting his infinite perfection in its multiple portrayals makes it easier for us to gain at least a preliminary understanding of that perfection.

By way of analogy, sunlight is "white" light, but it can be broken down when it is refracted through a prism. It is then "diversified" into the rainbow spectrum of seven visible colors—and some invisible ones like infrared and ultraviolet. Likewise, we can perceive, by divine revelation, only the tiniest glimpse of God's infinite essential perfection and never its undifferentiated oneness. By applying the "prism" of human intervention (theological analysis), we "artificially" diversify the divine omni-perfection and so can attain a limited grasp of it. That is the way we recognize it in our lives.

Thus, listing the divine attributes is really in some sense a fictional exercise. But the Lord graciously accommodates our human way of thinking about his superhuman status.

To elicit our response to his mercy more effectively, the Lord may present himself in many postures—for instance, as the Good Shepherd who seeks out and rescues his beloved lamb that has strayed into the brambles of sin. We can at any time bleat out our cry for help to our Good Shepherd and allow him to disentangle us from whatever thornbush into which we have plodded. Or we may see him and draw near to him as the Master who adroitly saved the adulteress from death by stoning. And ultimately we see the dying Christ extending mercy to the criminals on either side of him, as well as forgiveness to those who are executing him.

When we encounter the Lord in any of his postures of mercy, he is ready to hear our humble petition uttered in the spirit of the psalmist: "Hide your face from my sins, and blot out all my iniquities. Create in me a clean heart, O God, and put a new and right spirit within me" (Psalm 51:9–10). Immediately, if our repentance is authentic by virtue of our "firm purpose of amendment," we are made "pure of heart"—that is, soul-cleansed and assured that we are blessed: "Blessed are the pure in heart, for they will see God" (Matthew 5:8). Among other reasons, we are blessed because the damaging moral guilt or even the *feelings* of guilt (emotional guilt, formerly called a "guilt complex") no longer harass us.

Sincere repentance is the "delete button" on the keyboard of the soul. Once sin is deleted, nothing can revive that particular sin—although any future mistake (sin) will require another stroke of the "delete key" to again assure the soul's cleanliness. It is like the action of a car's windshield wiper, which cleanses repeatedly whether set to wipe frequently or with delays between strokes.

At the time of sincere repentance, *the soul should allow nothing to eclipse the conviction of its restored innocence* through Jesus' redeeming death. Consider Paul's forceful contention:

> Who will separate us from the love of Christ? Will hardship, or distress, or persecution, or famine, or nakedness, or peril, or sword?... No, in all these things we are more than conquerors.... For I am convinced that *neither death, nor life, nor angels, nor rulers, nor things present, nor things to come, nor powers, nor height, nor depth, nor anything else in all creation, will be able to separate us from the love of God in Christ Jesus our Lord.*" (Romans 8:35–39, italics mine)

FIVE

ROADBLOCKS TO MERCY: COUNTERFEIT REPENTANCE

God describes somewhat poetically through Isaiah the totality of sin remission: "I have swept away your transgressions like a cloud, and your sins like mist" (Isaiah 44:22). Notice, however, how the passage continues: "Return to me, for I have redeemed you." God requires that we undergo a *metanoia*—a repentance that entails a total conversion of heart.

Total forgiveness requires total repentance. It is only when our contrition extends to *all* of our recalled and even unrecalled offenses that he assures us that he "forgets" *all* of those failures, as Scripture reminds us repeatedly. Consider the words of the Lord through the prophet Ezekiel (18:21–22), with special emphasis on the initial "If." "[I]f the wicked turn away from all their sins that they have committed and keep all my statutes and do what is lawful and right, they shall surely live; they shall not die. None of the transgressions that they have committed shall be remembered against them."

The "condition of contrition" is spelled out with more detail in another passage, Ezekiel 33:15–16: "If the wicked restore the pledge, give back what they have taken by robbery, and walk in the statutes of life, committing no iniquity—they shall surely live.... None of the sins that they have committed shall be remembered against them." This implies an intent to not slide back into sin.

Thus, one major roadblock to God's mercy is the lack of a "firm purpose of amendment," to use an old catechetical term. But it may be asked, if "all have sinned and fall short of the glory of God" (Romans 3:23), and no one expects to remain sinless for the rest of his or her life, how can anyone have authentic repentance?

The full theological answer is, of course, that the awareness of our weakness and of probable future failure is an act of the *intellect*. The act of the *will*—that is, one's intent—is what matters morally. With the will we must sincerely *intend* never to sin again, even though we know with our intellect that future failures, though presently unintended, may occur.

Perverted minds may try to twist the meaning of that theological statement, but the words of the traditional prayer called the "Act of Contrition" state the truth uncompromisingly: "I firmly *resolve*, with the help of your grace, to sin no more and to avoid the near occasions of sin." That firm purpose of amendment is the authenticating feature of true repentance and the key that opens the floodgates of God's mercy on us.

Resistance to repentance is one abuse, but there is another and more subtle roadblock to being open to God's mercy. It is exemplified by pious people who have no deep awareness of their impoverished spiritual state—who feel that they have "no sins to confess." These people can't understand why Pope John Paul II availed himself of sacramental confession several times every week, as did some of the holiest of saints.

People who "have no sins to confess" might never think of confessing a lack of perfect conformity to God's will in hardships or failure to embrace generously and joyfully all physical, emotional and spiritual suffering. Neither do they feel the need to confess their neglect of various biblical injunctions, such as *rejoicing* in insults and persecution (Matthew 5:12); actually loving one's ene-mies—not just refraining from hating them (Luke 6:27, 35); lending without expecting repayment (Luke 6:35); not demanding the return of stolen goods (Luke 6:30-34) and so forth. They overlook—and hence never repent of—hundreds of daily faults that they can't even recognize as faults.

They seem to claim for themselves Voltaire's cynical statement, "The safest course is to do nothing against one's conscience. With this secret, we can enjoy life and have no fear from death."[1]

Saint John gives better advice:

If we say that we have no sin, we deceive ourselves, and the truth is not in us. If we confess our sins, he who is faithful and just will forgive us our sins and cleanse us from all unrighteousness. If we say that we have not sinned, we make him a liar, and his word is not in us. (1 John 1:8–10)

Think about that last sentence: If by sin-denial we make God a liar, that is itself a sin!

Such spiritual arrogance (or, in some cases, the lack of deep insight or self-perception) shows the need for a generous outpouring of the Holy Spirit's gift of fear of the Lord, a holy dread of offending the majesty of the Deity. "Those who fear the Lord prepare their hearts, and humble themselves before him" (Sirach 2:17). Conscience sensitivity reflects exquisite reverence for the majesty of God in the face of our frail human nature.

Conversion requires *convincing of sin* through the Holy Spirit's intervention. "And when he comes, he will prove the world wrong about sin and righteousness and judgment," Jesus said (John 16:8). Hence conversion renews and perfects the interior judgment of conscience.

No one can recall all the sins of one's life, so how can we confess and repent of all of our sins? The Council of Trent answered that question in the sixteenth century. Referring to sacramental confession, the Council stated that, through confessing all the sins that one can honestly remember, a penitent *implicitly* places *all* of his or her sins before the Divine Mercy for pardon.

But to deliberately withhold any sin would be to present nothing to God for his forgiveness. It would show a lack of total sincerity in repentance and a rejection of the *fullest* outpouring of God's mercy, which urges us to "be earnest, therefore, and repent" (Revelation 3:19). If one is too ashamed to show his wound to the doctor, it can't be healed. Surgery can heal only if the diseased area is exposed.

A person who bakes a cake but forgets to mix in the

eggs may produce a somewhat edible dessert but probably not a really delicious or attractive one. Likewise, a
person who sincerely decides to turn away from sin and
sinful habits might make a good initial start to a spiritual
rehabilitation, but something of the recipe may be missing: namely, the completion of the *metanoia*, which
requires not just turning away from sin but also turning to
the Lord.

Thus a real "change of heart" is not just a turning off
the hell-bound road but a complete turnaround on that
road. Your road of life may seem fine, but make sure
you're going in the right direction. Oprah Winfrey, an
unexpected source, restated that principle in a rather
whimsical fashion: "Failure is God's way of saying,
'Excuse me, you're moving in the wrong direction.'"[2]

Think of the decision to repent as threefold, not
twofold. It's not just a matter of choosing between sin and
no sin but also a matter of seeking the Lord as the be-all
and end-all of one's very existence. On a ladder scale the
choices would be sin (negative), no sin (neutral) and
virtue (positive). To stop at the second rung of the ladder,
no sin, would not be a complete *metanoia*. It would be radical justification but not complete justification, which
entails sanctification also.

The ladder analogy applies also to the norms for relating to one's enemy: hatred (negative); lack of hatred (neutral) and love (positive)—meaning simply the desire for
the "enemy's" overall welfare. The third response is the
one Jesus requires of Christians: "Love your enemies and
pray for those who persecute you" (Matthew 5:44). It is
the response that requires the Holy Spirit's enabling.

In the simplest terms, turning *from* sin is a counterfeit form of repentance if it does not include the intention of turning *to* God (see *CCC*, #1431, 2018). Like "the emperor's new clothes," something is missing in a casual diversion rather than radical turnaround from sin. If this is true for you, try shopping at Paul's haberdashery: "Clothe yourselves with the new self, created according to the likeness of God in true righteousness and holiness" (Ephesians 4:24).

This subject of "counterfeit repentance" is a very important one, one that needs to be developed thoroughly and theologically. The complaint of the Lord in Hosea 4:6, "My people are destroyed for lack of knowledge," has an urgency in all areas of God's word but especially in this topic of triggering the outpouring of Divine Mercy through repentance. I shall attempt to provide this knowledge in a reasonably orderly fashion in the next chapter.

SIX

SEVEN MISUNDERSTANDINGS ABOUT REPENTANCE

A classic letter from an anonymous taxpayer to the IRS stated, "My conscience won't let me sleep because I cheated on my tax payment. I am enclosing fifty dollars of the amount I owe you. If I still can't sleep, I'll send the rest."

Reminders of guilt torment the conscience. A church-sponsored billboard read, "YOU MUST PAY FOR YOUR SINS." Tempering these dire words was a forgiving graffito scrawled beneath them: "If your bill is already paid, please disregard this notice."

The bill for our sins, of course, *has* been paid already. Etymologically, the word *redemption* implies payment. The New Testament reminds us that we were "bought with a price" (1 Corinthians 6:20; 7:23), "with the precious blood of Christ" (1 Peter1:19; see also Acts 20:28).

Jesus proclaimed that he came "to give his life a ransom [the price of a slave] for many" (Matthew 20:28). But why the word *many*? Paul wrote that Christ "desires *everyone* to be saved" and so "gave himself as a ransom for *all*" (1 Timothy 2:4, 6, italics mine). Is everyone saved or only many? Or even less than many, as Jesus' words would imply: "The gate is narrow and the road is hard that leads to life, and there are few who find it" (Matthew 7:14; see Luke 7:24)?

Christ's ransom payment was "a bank deposit"—more than enough to pay for all. Yet not everyone will be saved because, like any bank deposit, redemption is accessible only to those who draw on it. How do we draw on it? By properly *repenting of all sin*.

Jesus himself affirms that condition for salvation: "Unless you repent, you will all perish" (Luke 13:3, 5). Yet as Peter wrote, "The Lord…is patient with you, not wanting *any* to perish, but *all* to come to repentance" (2 Peter 3:9, italics mine). And Paul told the pagan Athenians, "God…commands *all* people everywhere to repent" (Acts 17:30). As a noble people, they would have been moved at Alexander Pope's epigram: "A noble mind disdains not to repent."[1]

Thus, since "repentance…leads to salvation" (2 Corinthians 7:10), it is critically important. We should not delay the "repentance that leads to life" (Acts 11:18). As one quipster phrased it, "You can't repent too soon, because you don't know how soon it may be too late." But also repentance must be neither deficient nor improperly understood. Too often it is.

What Repentance Is Not

Many sincere but confused persons use substitutes for true repentance. A careful analysis of sinners' reactions to

their sins reveals at least seven possible ways of miscon-
struing what true repentance is. By reviewing and dis-
cussing these seven things that repentance is *not*, I hope to
clarify what authentic repentance actually is.

1) Repentance is not simply "practicing religion." As a
Puritan once remarked, "Even Judas heard Christ's ser-
mons." The Pharisees and Sadducees faithfully "practiced
religion" but neglected to produce "fruits worthy of
repentance" (Luke 3:8). They claimed that their status as
children of Abraham was enough for their spiritual security. But John the Baptist, baptizing "with water for repentance," saw their hypocrisy and called them a "brood of
vipers" (Matthew 3:7–9; Luke 3:7–9). As it's been said,
true religion comforts the afflicted but also afflicts the
comfortable.

**2) Repentance is not simply professing the faith of
Christianity.** Philip baptized Simon the sorcerer and
awed him with his miraculous powers (see Acts 8:13). But
Peter admonished Simon, "Your heart is not right before
God." *Repent*, for "I see that you are full of bitterness and
held captive by sin" (22–23, NLT).

Many Christians today also harbor bitterness and
resentment and are "captive to sin"—that is, under
bondage to sins such as marital infidelity, the use of arti-
ficial birth control, sexual sins, accepting the atrocity of
abortion, reading astrology columns and so on. Their
"cafeteria Christianity"—choosing only what they want
from doctrines and moral norms—tricks them into
thinking that they have true faith. Saint James, however,
points out that "even the demons believe—and shudder"

(James 2:19). Paul says that the person who repeatedly refuses to heed warnings "is perverted and sinful, being self-condemned" (Titus 3:11).

3) Repentance is not merely being convicted of one's sins—although this is an essential component. Jesus reminds us in John 16:8 that the Holy Spirit himself convicts us of sin—that is, convinces us of our guilt. The crafty teachers of the law and the Pharisees who wanted to stone the adulteress must have been convicted by their consciences when Jesus announced, "Let anyone among you who is without sin be the first to throw a stone at her" (John 8:7). Silently slinking away, one at a time, I suspect they were "convicted" but not truly repentant. After all, a true repentance turns one *toward* Jesus, not away from him.

4) Repentance is not based on natural motives. A "worldly" form of sorrow—that is, mere regret, natural remorse or shame for sin—is not enough. Paul gave the Corinthians an important teaching about two kinds of sorrow for sin (neither kind is *full* repentance, in itself, but one kind can lead to repentance):

> [Y]our grief led to repentance; for you felt a godly grief.... For godly grief produces repentance that leads to salvation and [therefore] brings no regret, but worldly grief produces death.... For see what earnestness this godly grief has produced in you, what eagerness to clear yourselves, what indignation [at wickedness], what alarm [at sin's danger], what longing, what zeal, what punishment [readiness to see justice done]. (2 Corinthians 7:9–11)

Thus Paul teaches that compunction for a failing could be either a natural or a supernatural form of remorse. Natural remorse ("worldly sorrow" or false repentance) arises from the experience of, or dread of, suffering in this life that results from sin, rather than the fact that God has been offended. This "worldly sorrow" is experienced by persons like the conscience-stricken tax dodger mentioned at the beginning of this chapter and the intemperate drinker who is sorry because of his hangover, or embarrassment at his drunken behavior or being fined or jailed for drunk driving.

Others give us examples of "worldly grief": the thief who regrets only that he got caught, the adulterer who regrets only the shattering of his marriage and the subsequent child support costs and the glutton who regrets only the bodily damage that results from his sin. Such "sorrow" is as spurious as the "crocodile tears" shed by the reptile in its "grief" for its devoured prey.

Scripture abounds in examples of such shallow repentance. The pharaoh expressed merely natural remorse (fear of resultant natural suffering) when he told Moses to "[p]ray to the LORD to take away the frogs from me and my people" (Exodus 8:8). The Israelites showed this form of defective repentance for their rebellion when they begged Moses to ask God to stop the punishing plague of venomous snakes (Numbers 21:7). King Jeroboam pleaded with the prophet to beg God to restore his instantly withered hand (1 Kings 13:6). Simon the sorcerer showed a false repentance (merely natural remorse), even in asking for Peter's atoning prayers, because he feared impoverishment by Peter's imprecation: "May your silver perish with you, because you thought you could obtain God's gift with money!" (Acts 8:20).

Even when asking others to pray for God to lift the punishment due to sin, such "worldly sorrow" is usually merely self-pity. Godly sorrow, on the other hand, comes by grace. This supernatural remorse will lead you to "repent…in the name of Jesus Christ" (Acts 2:38), while being aware that it is the Lord who "bless[es] you by turning each of you from your wicked ways" (3:26). Godly sorrow is aware that "God's kindness is meant to lead you to repentance" (Romans 2:4).

But this supernatural remorse lends itself to yet another distinction. If it focuses on God's justice in his wrath, it is called "attrition" or "imperfect contrition"; if it focuses on God's goodness, which draws us to love him, then it is "perfect contrition." Saint John explains this distinction implicitly in his fear-versus-love-motivation passage: "There is no fear in love, but perfect love casts out fear, for fear has to do with punishment, and whoever fears has not reached perfection in love" (1 John 4:18).

To have "not reached perfection in love" is to be *imperfect*. Hence the catechetical term "imperfect contrition." Those whose love for God is the motivating factor in their regret for sin have "perfect contrition"—that which validates the most meritorious form of repentance. Walter Hilton intuited this aspect of contrition: "When thou attackest the roots of sin, fix thy thought upon the God whom thou desirest rather than upon the sin which thou abhorrest."[2]

Yet even "imperfect contrition"—precisely because it is

not "worldly" but godly or supernatural—is sufficient for
the valid reception of the Catholic sacrament of reconciliation or penance (commonly called confession). *Both*
forms of "godly" or supernatural contrition are expressed
in the wording of the Catholic formula for the Act of
Contrition: "Because I dread your just punishments
[imperfect contrition], but *most of all*, because I have
offended you, My God, who are all good and deserving of
all my love [perfect contrition]."

5) Repentance is not presumed freedom from guilt.
Such a presumption is prideful self-righteousness, typi-
fied by the prayer of the Pharisee in Jesus' parable: "He
prayed about himself: 'God, I thank you that I am not like
other people: thieves, rogues, adulterers.... I fast twice a
week; I give a tenth of all my income'" (Luke 18:11–12).
We see the counterpoint of that mentality in the simple
prayer of the tax collector, "God, be merciful to me, a
sinner" (verse 13). If our repentance lacks humility, it is
not authentic repentance. Hence Jesus closes the parable
with the paradox: "[A]ll who exalt themselves will be
humbled, but all who humble themselves will be exalted"
(verse 14).

James reinforces this theme: "Draw near to God, and he
will draw near to you. Cleanse your hands, you sinners,
and purify your hearts, you double-minded.... Humble
yourselves before the Lord, and he will exalt you" (James
4:8, 10). Old Testament advice parallels this norm: "[I]f
my people...humble themselves, pray, seek my face, and
turn from their wicked ways, then I will hear from
heaven, and will forgive their sin" (2 Chronicles 7:14).

A surprising number of people cannot even get to the point of acknowledging their own guilt. I think of the lady in a fender-bender accident who berated the other motorist, "Why can't you drivers watch where you're going? You're the fourth person I crashed into today!" Carlyle wrote: "The deadliest sins were the consciousness of no sin."[3]

6) Repentance is not simply acknowledgment of one's sin. Failure to acknowledge guilt is one fault Judas didn't have. After betraying Jesus he went back to the chief priests and elders with his thirty pieces of silver and admitted explicitly: "I have sinned by betraying innocent blood." However, his admission of sin obviously did not equate with true repentance, for he despaired and "went and hanged himself" (see Matthew 27:3–5).

In fact, Judas Iscariot manifested most of the prerequisites of repentance. He certainly acknowledged his sin; he also had conviction of sin (awareness of a need to receive forgiveness); he had "religion" as a Christian, a follower of Christ; he had faith, at least from having witnessed Jesus' miracles; he restored the thirty pieces of silver to the chief priests and elders; he even expressed sorrow and remorse. But to grieve over sin is one thing; to repent is another.

Judas' tragic end shows that he fell short of authentic repentance. His repentance was vitiated by his despair, which was his refusal to accept the loving, compassionate mercy of God, a refusal that is one form of the "unforgivable sin." Loving mercy was offered to him up to the end, for Jesus called Judas "friend" at the very moment his lips were blistered with a traitorous kiss (see Matthew 26:50). Judas' despair crushed within him the virtue of hope and rendered useless all the prerequisites of repentance that he met.

7) Repentance without a firm purpose of amendment is not genuine repentance. Martin Luther once said, "To do it no more is the truest repentance."[4] But is this ideal possible?

Someone has opined that the only persons who don't sin are those who lie in the cemetery. The just don't stop sinning, but they rebound from their failures. The proverb writer reminds us that "though they [the righteous] fall seven times, they will rise again" (Proverbs 24:16).

As I mentioned earlier, the Greek fathers of the church called this kind of radical turnaround (even though it may be required repeatedly) *metanoia*. It looks on the past with a weeping eye and on the future with a watchful eye. Hence a sincere intention to change elicits a double action: turning away from the sin and turning toward God. As pointed out in the previous chapter, repentance is not a detour but a U-turn.

Certainly no one *expects* to remain sinless for the rest of his or her life, but anyone can sincerely *intend* to remain sinless. Sincerity is couched in the will, not the intellect. The intellect sees realistically the possibility of future failure, but in spite of this, the will can intend honestly (resolve) not to fail again. It helps to rethink often the capstone of the beautiful Catholic formula of the Act Contrition. Note the act of the will (resolution): "I firmly resolve, with the help of your grace, to sin no more and to avoid the near occasions of sin."

A backwoods preacher once said that sin is like capturing a bobcat up in a tree. "Ya don't need much he'p to catch 'im, but ya shore need lots o' he'p to make him leggo!" Letting go of habitual sin requires graces, given only to truly repentant souls with a firm purpose of amendment.

In the term *firm purpose of amendment*, the key word is *firm*. Unless one has a consistently firm resolve, one's sincerity can be questioned. Saint Francis de Sales wrote, "Weak, lazy penitents abstain regretfully from sin for a while. They would very much like to commit sins if they could do so without being damned."[5] That type of resolve is fear-based and not firm enough to validate "perfect" contrition or deep repentance.

In describing strong resolve, Saint Augustine said, "We make a ladder out of our vices if we trample those same vices underfoot."[6] Yet in some way there is an element of gradualism in this progression. Intuiting this, Henry Ward Beecher observed, "Repentance is another name for aspiration.... Repentance may begin instantly, but reformation often requires a sphere of years."[7]

So What Is Repentance?

Each of the above defective forms of repentance entails one essential requisite for true repentance, although each is in itself incomplete—incapable of constituting the kind of repentance that "leads to salvation" (2 Corinthians 7:10), though taken together they do. Each one lacks a proper *attitude*.

To make that picture more focused, let us use the analogy of driving a car. Driving presumes certain preconditions, as does true repentance, to reach one's destination:

1. The driver must have access to a car. The sinner must have access to a supportive religion as a "vehicle."

2. The driver should use the best route to reach his destination. The knowledgeable penitent knows the "Jesus route" (Christianity), for Jesus is the premiere "Way" (John 14:6).

3. The driver must recognize when he has taken a wrong turn; otherwise he can't correct it and will go farther afield. Likewise, the sinner must recognize ("be convicted") that he can change and needs to change a wrongful act or habit.

4. The driver usually feels frustrated at having made a wrong turn and regrets having done so. A sinner needs to have a proper sorrow or regret for each "wrong turn" (sin).

5. A driver, after a wrong turn, might have to humbly ask directions and apologize to his passengers for the delay. A sinner must humbly accept blame for his sin before God, asking his pardon without evasiveness, denial or self-righteousness.

6. A driver, when tagged by a police officer, should acknowledge his mistake when he has broken any traffic laws. A sinner, like the Prodigal Son, must say to God, "Father, I have sinned against heaven and before you; I am no longer worthy" (Luke 15:21).

7. The corrected driver must resolve sincerely to do his utmost to avoid future violations of any traffic laws. And the sinner must have a firm purpose of amendment (resolve) to avoid possible sin in the future.

In all of this it is clear that the role of one's interior attitude, not just one's exterior comportment, is of utmost importance. "[R]end your hearts and not your clothing. Return to the LORD, your God" (Joel 2:13). The Lord isn't interested in mere apologies. He looks for a heart broken not by sin itself but by the realization of the impact of sin on God—a heart broken not only for sin but also *from* sin. And for him to fix that broken heart, one must give him all the pieces.

The real meaning of "repentance that leads to salvation" is, at its heart, a *metanoia* turnaround. When we change from being sin-bound to being God-bound, a triple effect is produced: strength to resist future temptation, the removal of arrogant self-assurance in our pursuit of holiness and an increase of humble God-dependency.

Finally, an upbeat observation: All seven qualities of repentance are fulfilled by anyone who deeply loves God. Remember Saint Augustine's famous maxim, "*Deum ama et fac quod vis*" ("Love God, and do what you will").[8]

Both theology and God's word convey all of this cogently and urgently: "Cast away from you all the transgressions that you have committed against me, and get yourselves a new heart and a new spirit!" (Ezekiel 18:31). When we do that, God's merciful love dispels the evil of sin in our heart, as the radiant bursting dawn erases the darkness of night. With that, heaven is only a heartbeat away!

SEVEN

THE SPOT REMOVER FOR SIN-SOILED SOULS

As a youngster I thought that it was practically a law that every pet dog must be named Spot. That misconception was probably derived from the fact that all the dogs in our neighborhood had that name. In view of that bit of childhood history, I probably had a better-than-average laugh response to a TV comedian's quip that he put spot remover on his dog and the little cur disappeared!

I'm sure you can see the follow-up remark coming, but I have to affirm it anyway (the maxim of stand-up comedians: "Monologues go better with epilogues"). The Almighty's unique "spot remover" is, of course, his quick forgiveness. Sin-removing is the Lord's standard response to any heartfelt utterance of the acme of all petitions: "Forgive us our trespasses."

Someone, probably a clever televangelist, coined a quirky definition for the virtue of trusting in God's merciful love: he called it the "bathtub of the soul." A bath or shower restores a soiled body with an awareness of refreshing cleanliness; a sense of the absolute cleanliness of one's soul is even more refreshing and delightful. All the faces of trust, such as trust in God's answer to prayer, trust in his provision for one's financial security, trust in healing from the Lord and so on are all ultimately forms of dependence on God's mercy (as I explain in my book *Pathways of Trust: 101 Shortcuts to Holiness*). Yet there's no form of trust more fulfilling than trusting in God's mercy to cleanse us totally from sin.

That's why Jesus, in an apparition to Saint Faustina, commissioned her to propagate devotion to Divine Mercy through the devout use of that simple and trenchant ejaculation, "Jesus, I trust in you." In affirming trust in his forgiveness—the kind of trust Jesus responds to most eagerly—the petitioner implicitly affirms trust in his mercy in all of its many other expressions. The devotion to the Divine Mercy is meaningless without trust.

The human conscience performs a double sin-related function: our "prior conscience" tells us to avoid sin, and our "posterior conscience" tells us to be remorseful of sin. One says, "Don't do that!" and the other says, "Now you've done it!" In one single passage Saint John speaks of this double role of human conscience: "My little children, I am writing these things to you so that you may not sin. But if anyone does sin, we have an advocate with the Father, Jesus Christ the righteous" (1 John 2:1).

Both the "prevent" and the "repent" functions in a well-formed conscience are within the ambience of the merciful love of God, which we should prayerfully implore. He wants to extend his mercy to us by giving graces to prevent sin as well as graces to repent of sin.

Most Christians appreciate God's mercy in forgiving their sins, but they seldom thank him for the countless times that his merciful love has provided the grace (or fortitude) to avoid sinning when confronted with temptation. "[H]is mercies never come to an end; they are new every morning" (Lamentations 3:22–23). This is a forgotten aspect of his "abounding love"—a phrase often used in reference to the Lord's merciful love: "[Y]ou, O Lord, are good and forgiving, abounding in steadfast love to all who call on you" (Psalm 86:5).

Every thinking adult, civilized or savage, has a consciousness of sin, whether confessed or unconfessed. "All have sinned" (Romans 3:23; 5:12). Sin carries with it an intuitive dread of punishment or retribution.

In multifarious ways humankind has always attempted to cope with real or imagined guilt. People have tried self-flagellation, sleeping in coffins, spilling out their innermost humiliating secrets to psychiatrists, psychopathic masochism, starvation-like fasting, ceremonial crucifixion, engaging in endless hours of self-focused meditation, arduous pilgrimages and crusades, becoming hermits; the attempt to erase guilt, motivated either consciously or subconsciously, has taken literally thousands of forms over many centuries. None of these humanly engineered forms of guilt-erasure has been found to be truly satisfactory.

It's time now, in this age of mercy, for all to accept the fullness of God's plan for dissolving guilt. The Bible declares this with crystal clarity: "While God has overlooked the times of human ignorance, now he commands all people everywhere to repent" (Acts 17:30).

"[R]epentance and forgiveness of sins is to be proclaimed in his name to all nations" (Luke 24:47). Only persons who trustingly obey God's commanded method of sin-dissolving, as stated in his Holy Word, have found success in this otherwise futile venture: "Repent,... every one of you in the name of Jesus Christ so that your sins may be forgiven" (Acts 2:38).

All sin, including that which offends our fellow humans, is ultimately an offense against God—a violation of his will as perceived (often inadequately) by the human conscience. Sin is therefore a rupture in a relationship between a rational (conscience-responsive) creature and his or her Creator.

A conscience is either well-formed or malformed and can either accuse or excuse any given person, as Paul states (see Romans 2:15). (Inculpable ignorance can excuse one also.) In its accusatory form conscience operates—as explained earlier—either as "prior" conscience, reining us in, or "posterior" conscience, spawning a guilt feeling for wrongs already done. In one case we should trust God to help us avoid sin, and in the other case we should *trust* him to forgive our sin.

Because it is a personal relationship that is ruptured by sin, the restoration must be a very direct one-to-one, *personal* act. We can't relate personally to some impersonal or sub-personal cosmic "force" or entity. Divine revelation shows us that our God is a personal God, incredibly loving and merciful and far more eager to forgive us creatures than we are eager to be forgiven. Yet he requires us to be open to his proffered loving forgiveness; the faith act of accepting it is precisely an act of trust in his mercy.

All of this makes it consummately easy, even in a flashing moment, to be totally exonerated, relieved of all guilt. No self-scourging or other self-imposed hardships are required. It's simply a matter of soul-regret (remorse for having offended a loving God) and then surrender to his forgiving love, made meaningful for us by the sufferings of his Son, Jesus. In this context trust in his mercy is the most beneficial act of personalized faith possible. It confirms, up to that moment, one's very salvation.

It's heartening to know that something so necessary as salvation is so easy. Salvation is simply trusting God to manage our sins, just as we trust him to manage the supply of the air we breathe, the movement of atoms throughout the cosmos or the rising of the sun. Of the thousands of ways of attempting to attain true freedom from guilt and authentic peace, the *only* workable one is totally trusting the Lord. He dissolves our sins in his merciful love, like tissue paper in a blast furnace.

> [I]f the wicked turn away from all their sins that they have committed and keep all my statutes and do what is lawful and right…[n]one of the transgressions that they have committed shall be remembered against them.… Have I any pleasure in the death of the wicked, says the Lord GOD, and not rather that they should turn from their ways and live? (Ezekiel 18:21–23)

A reliance on Christ's sin-atonement brings about a Christlike peace—one that transcends any worldly imitation of tranquility: "Peace I leave with you; my peace I give to you. I do not give to you as the world gives. Do not let your hearts be troubled" (John 14:27). But the moment we stop trusting him, we are left to drown in a sea of guilt. So let him wash those sins away!

EIGHT

GO TO HELL—BUT ONLY IF YOU CHOOSE TO GO

I n a nasty political argument a Massachusetts senator shouted at his colleague the vicious epithet, "Go to hell!" The insulted politician asked the governor (and future president) Calvin Coolidge to do something about it. Coolidge calmly replied, "I have looked up the law, Senator, and I assure you, you don't have to go."[1]

Nor does anyone. Any soul can choose to fashion its own eternity. "I have set before you life and death, blessings and curses. Choose life so that you...may live" (Deuteronomy 30:19).

The greatest love story the world has ever known is the paradoxical drama of a God who loves enough to hate evil. He loves us sinners as his precious children, and he hates our sin because it is the evil that poisons us. So in the book of Judges and elsewhere it is recorded that he disciplined Israel repeatedly in efforts to entice his people to abandon idolatry.

God cares enough to be angry with the trivializing of evil and the refusal to acknowledge the need for his mercy. He cares enough to be angry with the devil-inspired distortion of evil as mere petty legalism. The Lord protests, "I have no pleasure in the death of the wicked, but that the wicked turn from their ways and live" (Ezekiel 33:11).

Amazingly, as angry as God is with the sins of humankind, he came not to condemn: "God did not send the Son into the world to condemn the world, but in order that the world might be saved through him" (John 3:17), for "God our Savior…desires everyone to be saved and to come to the knowledge of the truth" (1 Timothy 2:3–4).

Because God revealed himself in the mirror image of his Son (see Colossians 1:15), in Jesus we find an accurate picture of the balance between God's love for us and his wrath toward evil. He loved us enough to warn us of pending judgment (see Matthew 25:31–46), while assuring us that his love is equal to his hatred of sin: "God so loved the world that he gave his only Son, so that everyone who believes in him may not perish but may have eternal life" (John 3:16). Jesus loved enough to overturn the tables of the money changers desecrating the sacred temple (Matthew 21:12).

Any father is angry at the disease that ravages the body of his sick child. So does God detest the moral sickness called evil or sin that contaminates his dear children, whom he loves most tenderly. "As a father has compassion for his children, so the LORD has compassion for those who fear [reverence] him" (Psalm 103:13). "I have come to call not the righteous but sinners to repentance," said Jesus (Luke 5:32).

We cannot afford to misunderstand the relationship between the love and justice of God. Pope John Paul II, in his encyclical *Dives in Misericordia*, wrote that "justice alone is not enough" to correct the ailing world. We need God's mercy, and we need to be transmitters of that mercy to convert those deserving of justice.[2] That sublime thought might be stated simply as "Many persons who cry loudly for justice would soon beg for mercy instead, if justice were done to them."

Jesus did not come to condemn us but to save us from our sin and from destruction by the infernal punisher, into whose hands our unrepented sin would drive us. Jesus said, "Do not fear those who kill the body but cannot kill the soul; rather fear him who can destroy both soul and body in hell" (Matthew 10:28). The truth is that God's mercy is infinite and equal to his justice. Yet he seeks to apply his mercy to prevent the need for his justice.

There's a not-so-ecumenical joke about an Irish Catholic cop who stopped a priest who was exceeding the speed limit. He said, "Father, I stopped you to tell you that there's a Protestant cop at the next corner."

It's a schmaltzy yarn, but it provides a humorous way of formulating the principle that mercy can override justice without denying justice, and mercy can also prevent the need for justice to be applied.

Because of God's love he found a way to show mercy. His hatred of sin will not bring down his wrath as long as his mercy isn't spurned. The poetic and touching dictum of Charles Sprague says, "Hate shuts her soul when dove-eyed Mercy pleads."[3] That is, the Lord pleads gently and lovingly, urging us to avoid the tragic choice of our own eternal punishment that we would bring upon ourselves.

When Saint Rose of Lima suffered doubts about her salvation, Jesus appeared to her and reassured her that he condemns only those who choose to be condemned by refusing to repent. Saint Thomas Aquinas says that only those who refuse God's forgiving love experience his punishing justice.[4] That's why we can say that God has never sent anyone to hell; the reprobate ones have chosen hell themselves by simply refusing to say sincerely, "I'm sorry." That simple apology to God is called repentance. It is the master switch that opens the floodgates of his mercy.

God chooses to "strike" with his pointing and beckoning finger, not with a punishing arm. Sometimes his "pointing finger" directs us to channels of his mercy that we have been neglecting to recognize. "Seek good and not evil, that you may live; and so the LORD...will be with you" (Amos 5:14).

The Lord stays with us, as he promised (Matthew 28:20). For instance, he is with us by a most loving presence in the Holy Eucharist. Perhaps we avail ourselves frequently of the Eucharist and yet forget that it is an exquisitely generous and veritably touchable source of his mercy, as well as a manifestation of it—both a cause and an effect of his mercy. Just think of the mercy component in the words of consecration: "This is my body...given for you.... This is my blood...shed for you." Or in Paul's words to the Corinthians: "The cup of blessing that we bless, is it not a sharing in the blood of Christ? The bread that we break, is it not a sharing in the body of Christ?" (1 Corinthians 10:16).

The most obvious mercy component of this sacrament is the salvific promise incorporated into its very reception: "Those who eat my flesh and drink my blood have eternal life, and I will raise them up on the last day" (John 6:54). Those words mean that for those who devoutly receive the eucharistic Lord Jesus, with faith in his substantive and real presence, he stakes a "Welcome" sign at the pearly gates. How's that for the ultimate offer of Divine Mercy?

In heaven's "priority list" of channels of Divine Mercy, a most prominent place has been assigned to Mary, some of whose many titles include "Mother of Mercy" and "Refuge of Sinners." Only three direct quotations of Mary are found in the Bible, but within those few sentences you'll find the word *mercy* twice: "His mercy is for those who fear [reverence] him" (Luke 1:50). And "He has helped his servant Israel, in remembrance of his mercy" (Luke 1:54).

Mary's intervention at the wedding feast of Cana triggered the first public miracle of her Son—itself an act of mercy designed to hide the embarrassment of the hosting celebrants. In her presence on Calvary she witnessed the greatest act of mercy ever—the torturous death of her Son, the God-man Jesus, whose passion she supported with her "com-passion."

Mary is the premiere instrument of God's mercy, for she gave the world its Redeemer and is now a disburser of the graces of redemption to us, her spiritual children, by her intercession before the presence of her Son in heaven, just as she mercifully interceded at Cana. Centuries of uninterrupted prayers for her intercession have redounded to countless bestowed benefits to humankind; they flow ultimately from the merciful heart of God, at her behest. Seasoned souls would never neglect to invoke the Mother of Mercy to intercede with the Lord for a copious outflow of gifts of mercy from his bounteous heart.

God generously uses other creatures as instruments of his mercy: angels, saints, our beloved dead in heaven—and even those who may be still in a state of purgation, who ask for our mercy by prayer yet are chosen instruments of God's mercy to us by their prayers.

The Earth is full of God's instruments of mercy: supportive friends, missionaries, teachers, medical personnel, even animals. A Seeing Eye dog, for instance, is one of the most beautiful examples of God's earthly instruments of his compassionate mercy.

Any soul who chooses to reject, or at least not to acknowledge, the Divine Mercy in its countless facets blithely staggers toward eternal damnation, starved of the delicious fruits of grace and mercy that abound in the orchard through which he slogs in his life journey. For these our prayer is paradoxical: "Lord, before it's too late, have mercy on those who reject your mercy!"

NINE

THE PRISON CELL THAT'S NEVER LOCKED

A cartoon showed a bedraggled and disheveled prisoner probing his open cell door, calling to his gaunt cellmate, "The good news is that the cell door isn't locked. The bad news is that it never was—there's no keyhole!"

The truly bad news is that countless people imprison themselves for years at a time in their self-induced guilt, and the "worse" news is that they don't realize the "good" news that the Lord has provided an easy escape plan.

Why would anyone choose to live in a prison cell when not forced to? Or wallow in the sludge of oppressive, negative feelings of guilt when a simple cleansing of the filth is almost absurdly easy to reach? Imagine a person so dysfunctional that he shuts himself up in a dark, stuffy cave and closes the entrance so tightly that not the slightest ray of sunlight can penetrate the darkness. Would anyone blame the sun for that situation? A normal person would want to exclaim, "Open the entrance of your cave and let in some sunlight! Better still, come outside and enjoy basking in the brilliant warmth of this beautiful day!"

The good news is God's gift offered to every despondent heart: "In your presence there is fullness of joy" (Psalm 16:11). Our heavenly Father, in his indescribable divine love, can hardly wait to "forgive us our trespasses." The Holy Spirit inspired the prophet Micah to articulate this amazing truth as a question that contrasts our God with pagan gods: "Who is a God like you, pardoning iniquity and passing over the transgression?" (Micah 7:18).

God's loving mercy overrides his righteous indignation at the horrendous evil of sin (which is an act of insulting the Creator of the universe). When the sinner takes the tiniest step toward his waiting open arms, God embraces him with the warmest affection. Truly God's tenderness and love total far more than all the human love added up from the beginning of human existence on Earth.

Few will deny that God's wisdom and power are infinite—although no one can really grasp them. But God's infinite mercy is a concept that many prisoners of their own guilt find hard to appreciate. As Paul says, "In their case the god of this world has blinded the minds of the unbelievers, to keep them from seeing the light of the gospel" (2 Corinthians 4:4). They can't accept the simple procedure required for eternal salvation: "Repent therefore, and turn to God so that your sins may be wiped out" (Acts 3:19).

The self-imprisoned may be unaware of the "no-keyhole door." In fact, any sinner's "cell" has a number of unlocked doors to afford him or her escape from the confinement of sin. The Bible speaks of six such portals of God's mercy—three of which are sacraments. *But implied for each one is the prerequisite of a repentant heart.*

PORTALS OF MERCY

First, of course, is the "start-off-clean" sacrament. Baptism removes original sin, which is "'contracted' and not 'committed'—a state and not an act" (*CCC*, #404). This is the sin that Romans 5:12 describes: "[S]in came into the world through one man, and so death spread to all because all have sinned."

The baptism of non-infants also remits personal sin: "Repent, and be baptized every one of you in the name of Jesus Christ so that your sins may be forgiven" (Acts 2:38).

The second portal of mercy is the sacrament of reconciliation (improperly called "confession," which is only the penitent's act of relating his sins to the priest). This sacrament is the most perfect door of escape from the prison cell of sin, because Jesus instituted it precisely for that purpose alone. He arranged for it to be channeled only through the apostles and their clergy successors: "As the Father has sent me, so I send you.... If you forgive the sins of any, they are forgiven them; if you retain the sins of any, they are retained" (John 20:21–23).

Besides conferring God's "negative mercy"—sin removal—this sacrament also confers more of God's "positive mercy"—namely, a restoration or increase of sanctifying grace (see 2 Peter 1:4), a surge of actual grace to discern better what is sinful and be able to avoid it (Philippians 2:13), an inflow of sacramental grace that intensifies contrition (2 Corinthians 7:10), an increase of merit or heavenly reward (1 Corinthians 3:8), an added indulgence for the lessening or dissolving of accumulated purgatorial suffering (1 Corinthians 3:13–15) and finally, a special spiritual intimacy with Christ in his gentle mercy (Matthew 11:28).

Third, we have the portal of the sacrament of the anointing of the sick, which was formerly called extreme unction. "Are any among you sick? They should call for the elders of the church and have them pray over them, anointing them with oil in the name of the Lord…. [A]nd the Lord will raise them up; and anyone who has committed sins will be forgiven" (James 5:14–15).

Fourth, we enter the freedom of God's mercy through repentance, also known as contrition. Either "perfect" (based on love of God) or "imperfect" contrition (also called "attrition," based on fear of punishment) can educe forgiveness of sin. Even without sacramental confession and its many special advantages just listed, perfect contrition by itself suffices to remove mortal sin. However, ecclesiastical law, not divine law, requires that any such forgiven mortal sins be "submitted to the keys" of the church's power in the sacrament of reconciliation, if available, before receiving Communion. Meanwhile, if no confession is available, or if the sins are doubtfully mortal, Communion may be received after a preparation by perfect contrition (see CCC, #1452).

Imperfect contrition is not a sufficient preparation for Communion after mortal or doubtfully mortal sin. But with confession, imperfect contrition suffices to remove any sin. The Council of Trent affirmed all this (see *CCC*, #1453).

Fifth, an act of sincere love of God that would imply a deep regret of having offended him as the beloved of the soul also gives entrance to God's mercy. This act would contain implicitly an act of perfect contrition and hence would be conditioned by the above statements regarding perfect contrition. "I tell you, her sins, which were many, have been forgiven; hence she has shown great love. But the one to whom little is forgiven, loves little" (Luke 7:47).

Sixth, an act of sincere fraternal charity—that is, an act of love of God as his presence is recognized in another human—brings us to mercy in another way: "We know that we have passed from death to life because we love one another. Whoever does not love abides in death" (1 John 3:14). This Christ-focused fraternal charity also would contain perfect contrition implicitly and hence open us to the above conditions.

Given these six routes of "escape from the prison of sin," we can only marvel at how the Lord strives to give us every opportunity to be free of the bondage and confinement of sin. It seems that he strives to exhaust his divine ingenuity in finding ways to shower us with his loving mercy. All that is required of us is to reach out to him and be caught up in his embrace of mercy.

There's a bumper sticker that says, "If you feel far from God, guess who moved!" That is a reversible separation, as David showed in his simple prayer: "Draw near to me, redeem me, set me free" (Psalm 69:18). Yet countless souls have become calloused in not recognizing the Lord's yearning to embrace us in his mercy: "I took them up in

my arms; but they did not know that I healed them. I
led them with cords of human kindness, with bands
of love...like those who lift infants to their cheeks"
(Hosea 11:3–4).

A Merciful Encounter

A passenger next to me on a plane flight noticed my
Roman collar and soon engaged me in a conversation
about religion. He remarked that he had given up his
childhood faith "because," he said, "the Bible speaks so
much about the wrath of God." He was incredulous when
I told him that every such passage was qualified by the
option offered to every sinner to evade such wrath by
turning to God's mercy. I observed that the Bible men-
tions the mercy of God directly in more than four hundred places and indirectly in hundreds of other places,
from the psalm prayers to the mercy parables of Luke 15
and beyond.

When this man brought up the time-worn objection
about Jesus' referral to the "unforgivable sin," I explained
that *any sin that is "unforgivable" is not so by reason of God's
refusal to forgive but by the sinner's refusal to be forgiven*. The
sinner refuses forgiveness by simply refusing to apologize
to God for spitting in his face by sin. The Lord patiently
and lovingly urges the sinner to accept his divine forgiveness, but the recalcitrant sinner simply refuses to accept it.

I showed my fellow passenger a statement from the
Catechism, a copy of which, providentially, I happened to
have in my valise. I urged him to read not just the opening words of the passage but the entire paragraph. It
started with the words of Jesus: "I tell you, every sin and

blasphemy will be forgiven men, but the blasphemy against the Spirit will not be forgiven." Then followed the commentary: "There are no limits to the mercy of God, but anyone who deliberately refuses to accept his mercy by repenting, rejects the forgiveness of his sins and the salvation offered by the Holy Spirit. Such hardness of heart can lead to final impenitence and eternal loss" (CCC, #1864).

The third personality in God's triple personality, the Holy Spirit, acts as grace-bestower. Thus "blasphemy against the Spirit" is simply refusal to accept God's grace of forgiveness and salvation.

I tried explaining this by a simple kindergarten-level illustration: "If you were poor and I offered you a no-strings-attached gift of a million dollars and you refused it, could you blame me for selfishness or injustice? Your being deprived of the gift would be your choice, not mine. Counterpoint that example with the passage about the 'unforgivable sin,' coupled with the inspired words of Peter: 'The Lord is…patient with you, not wanting any to perish, but all to come to repentance' (2 Peter 3:9)."

The world's worst sinner can be forgiven in a fraction of a second by simply saying to the Lord, with true sincerity, "I'm sorry." Refusing to do so is the only way one can end up in hell. The unrepentant sinner says, in effect, that he is prepared to accept the endless anguish of hell rather than humble himself by opening up to God's mercy with a simple apology.

I showed my fellow passenger that instead of distortedly emphasizing the wrath of God, he should emphasize the pride and stupidity of any unrepentant sinner. The wrath of God is mentioned in the Bible *only* in the context of the obdurate and sustained refusal of persons or nations who snub his loving mercy.

The devil knows that pride is the main roadblock to repentance and ultimately salvation. "'God opposes the proud but gives grace to the humble.' Submit yourselves therefore to God.... Draw near to God, and he will draw near to you. Cleanse your hands, you sinners, and purify your hearts.... Humble yourselves before the Lord, and he will exalt you" (James 4:6–8, 10).

When I opened my Bible and showed the man just a few descriptions of God's tender mercy, such as the parable about the Prodigal Son, his acrimony seemed to melt away. I invited him to say, "I'm truly sorry, Lord," while accepting the salvation earned for him by Jesus' death. He hastened to blurt out that commitment—almost tearfully. His parting words as the plane landed were words of gratitude and a promise to return to the practice of his Christian faith. Truly, "the hope of the righteous ends in gladness" (Proverbs 10:28).

This encounter left me with a grateful heart too, as I recalled the words of James 5:20: "[W]hoever brings back a sinner from wandering will save the sinner's soul from death and will cover a multitude of sins."

TEN

MERCY IN COSMIC CAMOUFLAGE: PROVIDENCE AT WORK

Even for a weathered cattleman, watching cows forage on a countryside greensward would normally not evoke an awareness of God's merciful love—unless that stockman stopped to marvel at the fact that God must have had the animal-to-land ratio in mind when he created grasses. Why?

Because practically all grasses, unlike most vegetation, grow from the base, rather than from the tip. Thus grasses survive and continue to grow after animals graze, so that the same grassland can be grazed again later. God's Word hints at this ecological wonder: "[T]heir pasture lands shall be for their cattle, for their livestock, and for all their animals" (Numbers 35:3). Thus "he will bless…your grain,…the increase of your cattle and the issue of your flock" (Deuteronomy 7:13).

Providence simply means "providing." It is God's fatherly concern providing for his creation and ultimately for the welfare and survival of us, his cherished children—humankind at large. "For you love all things that exist, and detest none of the things that you have made.... [H]ow would anything not called forth by you have been preserved? You spare all things, for they are yours, O Lord" (Wisdom 11: 24–26).

Such compassionate, providential concern is one tiny aspect of God's omnipresent, merciful love for us. Providence is one of many forgotten aspects of his awesome mercy. To attempt to list and explain in detail even a tiny fraction of the cosmic outreaches of this loving Providence would be like trying to recount the fascinating genealogical history of every person listed in the Manhattan phone directory.

But consider for a moment a random choice: Everyone knows that hot air rises and cold air tends to sink. But God made another set of rules for water. As it freezes its molecules form a crystalline structure, which is an expanded (hence less dense) form. Thus the ice floats.

Without this reversal of the usual temperature pattern, frozen lakes would never thaw, and the oceans would become solid ice, with all marine life mummified forever. Without the Earth's life-sustaining hydrologic cycle (see Genesis 1:6–7), life as we know it would be impossible.

In designing the atomic components of water and their special molecular-level interaction, God's providence was already fashioning everything, lovingly, for our welfare. "The LORD is good to all, and his compassion is over all that he has made" (Psalm 145:9). This passage portrays the "positive" aspect of God's mercy, operating from the moment of the creation of the universe. This is another dimension of his goodness beyond his offer of sin-erasure.

At each step of creation "God saw that it was good" (Genesis 1:4, 12, 18, 21, 25, 31). It was good in itself by manifesting his glory and power, but it was good also for us in providing for the sustaining of our existence. His personal goodness behind all this is his altruistic concern for us, his creatures. Such "loving-kindness" (to use biblical verbiage), in the most momentous act of creating the universe, is one of the least heralded and yet most awesome aspects of the Creator's Divine Mercy. In contemplating this vast creation, the macrocosm from the perspective of an astronomer or the microcosm from the perspective of a microbiologist, one can't help but be overwhelmed by the wonders of nature.

Did you know, for instance, that human eyes have never seen the world's second highest mountain? A few feet lower than Mount Everest, it's twice as tall as the highest mountain in the continental United States. Discovered in 1953 by oceanographers sonar-mapping the Pacific Ocean floor, the pinnacle of this 28,500-foot mountain lies 1,200 feet below the ocean's surface—rising from the ocean bottom in the Tonga Trench between New Zealand and Samoa.

Many splendid wonders of creation lie submerged, unrecognized and for the most part unappreciated. As they are discovered, they should make us marvel even more at their source. The stupendous scope of God's merciful love creates, conserves and orchestrates the work of his hands. And far greater than all this, says Saint Thomas Aquinas, is his work of grace in any one human![1]

To foster the appropriate wonderment at God's providence, his word scintillates with superlative exclamations from the heart of the Creator: "I have loved you with an everlasting love; therefore I have continued my faithfulness to you" (Jeremiah 31:3). In their attempt to reciprocate this love, the great saints, whose mystical experiences have raised them to the dizzy heights of love-union with God, have learned to some degree how to become immersed in the ocean of his tenderness. They feebly strive—and fail—to articulate the experience of these encounters, amazed that they even survived them.

It was probably from such an encounter that Paul strove to express his steadfastness in clinging to the great gift of God's merciful love: "I am convinced that neither death, nor life, nor angels, nor rulers, nor things present, nor things to come, nor powers, nor height, nor depth, nor anything else in all creation, will be able to separate us from the love of God in Christ Jesus our Lord" (Romans 8:38–39). And he was granted a glimpse of mystical mountains of divine goodness awaiting us beyond this life: "[N]o eye has seen, nor ear heard, nor the human heart conceived, what God has prepared for those who love him" (1 Corinthians 2:9).

To know how lovely his love is, try immersing yourself in his mercy! You could start by "re-creating" the review of creation—his initial act of mercy, lifting creatures out of non-existence into existence. God stood back at each stage of his masterwork and "saw that it was good." He rejoiced and reveled in the handiwork of his omnipotence. I like to imagine myself standing next to him, viewing the cosmic panorama, like a carpenter's child holding his father's gnarled hand while admiring his accomplishment: "You did a good job, Daddy!" I can almost hear the angel choirs providing the background hymn, "How Great Thou Art!"

This "cosmic contemplation" will lead you to an awareness of the indescribable *joy of the Lord* in providing for his creatures' existence and care in every aspect: creation, redemption, forgiveness, healing—and more. It's a joy to see God rejoice. "[A]s the bridegroom rejoices over the bride, so shall your God rejoice over you" (Isaiah 62:5). "I will rejoice…, and delight in my people" (Isaiah 65:19). "The Lord, your God, is in your midst…; he will rejoice over you with gladness, he will renew you in his love; he will exult over you" (Zephaniah 3:17).

As you continue your "mercy-appreciation" fantasy, watching God enjoy himself, you'll even "make God smile!" And he invites you to come and "enter into the joy of your master" (Matthew 25:21). "I speak these things in the world so that they may have my joy made complete in themselves" (John 17:13). Maybe Voltaire, in spite of his humanism, understood this better than most Christians do: "God is a comedian," he said, "playing to an audience too afraid to laugh."[2]

There's more than enough biblical material to support your meditation on the mercy-based joy of the Lord, such as Jeremiah 32:41, "I will rejoice in doing good to them." His forgiving mercy provides a special joy for the Lord. Just recall his joy in each of the "mercy" parables of Luke 15. The man who finds the one lost sheep "lays it on his shoulder and rejoices" (verse 5). The woman who finds her coin calls her neighbors to "rejoice with me" (verse 9). The father lays a scrumptious feast for the returning Prodigal Son after ordering for him the best robe, ring and sandals (verses 22–24).

As you revel in the forgiveness that leaves your soul "spanking-clean," you might say, "The pleasure is mine"; and God will respond, "No, the pleasure is mine!" For "he delights in showing clemency" (Micah 7:18), even more than he delights in the marvels of the universe that he drew from the void of nothingness.

To Saint Faustina he revealed, "I rejoice that [trusting souls] ask for much, because it is my desire to give much, very much."[3] He stated that his forgiving mercy, when accepted by even the worst sinners, provides him with his greatest joy—far beyond the understanding that any human or even angelic mind could ever attain even through all eternity! The very cosmos isn't large enough to encompass that divine bliss. What joy can compare with that?

ELEVEN

GOD THINKS BIG—HE MADE ELEPHANTS, DIDN'T HE?

There's an oft-told anecdote about the great luminary of theological insight, Saint Augustine. One day, walking along the seashore, pondering the greatness of God and his boundless goodness and mercy, he came upon a tiny child at the water's edge, repeatedly dipping a spoon into the water and emptying it into a pail.

"Why are you doing that?" asked Augustine.

The child answered that he was trying to see if he could empty the entire ocean into the pail. Augustine patiently explained that it would be an impossible task. The child then revealed that he was an angel in human form, sent by God to teach the saint that it would be even more futile for any created mind to try to engulf the infinite ocean of God's goodness and mercy. With that the child vanished, leaving the great theologian profoundly humbled and awestruck.

The Curé of Ars, Saint John Vianney, who spent as much as sixteen hours a day in the confessional, preached that all the sins ever committed were like one tiny grain of sand in comparison to the huge mountain of God's mercy. If that truth were universally acknowledged, there would be no case of despair in all of human history, nor of shame-fostered depression or suicide, including that of Judas.

And yet, even in suicide and other tragedies reported in the news every day, the Lord doesn't withdraw his offer of mercy up to the last second of life—as long as there is a remote possibility of a sinful person's accepting it. After a neighbor's suicide Augustine speculated, "The mercy of God may be found between the bridge and the stream."[1]

Of course, to depend on such last-second miraculous intervention by God would be rash beyond words, entailing a most serious risk of eternal damnation. Augustine also said: "There is one case of deathbed repentance recorded, that of the penitent thief, that none should despair; and only one that none should presume."[2]

Jeremy Taylor underscored this risk in his elegiac way with words: "Mercy is like the rainbow, which God hath set in the clouds; it never shines after it is night. If we refuse mercy here, we shall have justice in eternity."[3]

The Scriptures reiterate the importance of prompt responses to grace. The author of Hebrews, quoting Psalm 95, cites this key teaching three times: "Therefore, as the Holy Spirit says, 'Today, if you hear his voice, do not harden your hearts as in the rebellion, as on the day of testing in the wilderness, where your ancestors put me to the test, though they had seen my works'" (Hebrews 3:7–9; see also 3:15; 4:7).

It must be kept in mind that any repentance that is merely a partial remorse for sin is not authentic repentance and will not draw down the fullness of God's merciful forgiveness. Judas confessed his treason but not his thievery and hypocrisy; his "repentance" was simply an anguished and despairing regret. If his repentance had been complete and sincere, it would have embraced all of his iniquity, and a Niagara Falls of God's mercy would have cleansed his soul. By contrast, when David was overcome by one sin, he renewed his repentance for all his sins in his prayer in Psalm 51: "Wash me thoroughly from my iniquity, and cleanse me from my sin" (verse 2).

God's triumphant remedy for sin-diseased souls involves radical surgery, not just a Band-Aid patch. When the Lord restores a soul, he wants to perform a complete overhaul. So if you have a "spiritual paralysis" in one hand, don't ask him to heal it while you hold out your other hand to the devil.

I like the quaint proverb, "Those who think small race their pet slugs on a one-yard track." Shortsighted souls think small; they are seldom heaven-focused in their worldview. They look at life through a microscope rather than a telescope. Such narrow-minded, self-focused people are more concerned about their dieting hardships than about the fact that every two seconds a person somewhere dies of starvation and that three-fourths of those starving are children.

But God thinks big. He made elephants, didn't he?

One of the least recognized advantages of trials and temptations is the plan of God to promote a broader work of grace in the soul. A homeowner will have the entire roof checked when even one leak is found. A homemaker will wash not just a stained section of a garment but the entire garment. So God is concerned for our entire spiritual welfare, not just a part of it. Hence, refusing to be open to this broad action of grace is to frustrate God's magnanimous plan for us, in our personal life and in our relationships with others.

The Almighty has designed his mercy to flow to us, his creatures, limitlessly in "quantity" and also in duration. Quantitatively it is inestimable, beyond words: "Who can measure his majestic power? And who can fully recount his mercies?" (Sirach 18:5). In duration it is simply eternal—"from everlasting to everlasting," without beginning and without end: "The steadfast love of the LORD never ceases, his mercies never come to an end" (Lamentations 3:22).

Though limitless in itself, God's mercy can be received expansively in some and truncated in others, just as various-sized containers can collect various amounts of rainwater. We probably know people who wallow in the disappointment of unanswered prayers, which often leads to a subtly diminished faith. Such people may then slip into the conviction that God isn't really all that eager to help them. They may begin to think that they have a "right" to what they ask for. Their prayers may become petulant, like the pleading of a recalcitrant and demanding child, who whines for every fancied toy on the store shelves.

The prayer of Daniel provides a prototype of the best way to draw down the fullest outpouring of Divine Mercy: "We do not present our supplication…on the ground of our righteousness, but on the ground of your great mercies" (Daniel 9:18). This recognition of infinite mercy on God's part and of our humble reliance on that mercy encompasses the very essence of petition prayer— and also the quintessence of Christian spirituality.

TWELVE

DIVINE MERCY AS A SIN VACCINE

Just as tumbleweeds propagate themselves by dropping their seeds as the wind blows them across the terrain, so also many souls, knowingly or not, spread their own species of hellish weed. They "tumble" through life with the unstable winds of conformity, leaving in the hearts of others the obnoxious effects of their wickedness—seeds of bad example, disillusionment from "unanswered" prayer, moral collapse from observed scandal or even malicious enticement to immoral acts.

Grace-protected souls, however, are not appropriate soil for such seeds of iniquity, for the Lord immunizes them in the face of the enemy's hell-inflamed frustration. What is the theological basis for speaking of God's mercy as a preventative "vaccine," and how does it immunize us?

As far back as the thirteenth century, we find this concept exposited theologically. In the Middle Ages Saint Thomas Aquinas called attention to the fact that one of the special characteristics of Divine Mercy is that it engenders in the soul a type of grace called "antecedent grace" (Aquinas actually called it "prevenient grace").[1] This grace is an act of God's favor that is supplied before we are even aware that we need it. Our hindsight is always God's foresight.

An interesting example of this can be seen in the diary of Saint Faustina. In reference to her saintly spiritual director, Father Michael Sopocko, she wrote: "I can see that Divine Providence had prepared him to carry out this work of mercy before I had asked God for this. Oh, how strange are your ways, O God! And how happy are the souls that follow the call of divine grace!"[2] Faustina probably had no knowledge about the theology of antecedent grace, but she experienced it frequently as an apparently normal flow of the Lord's goodness toward her.

It is part of the Lord's divine ingenuity that he has designed his mercy to operate in many and varied oblique ways. He sometimes uses one person's failure as a merciful way of forestalling similar failures in others. For example, witnessing the disaster of family fragmentation stemming from a neighbor's divorce can make other couples strive to restore their own deteriorating marital love by prayer, marriage counseling, marriage retreats, love-fostering dialogue, mutual compliments and so forth.

Scripture presents the faults as well as the victories of the heroes of our faith. Simply knowing that Moses, the meekest man of his time (see Numbers 12:3), was provoked to a fury (see Exodus 32:19) gives us pause to consider our own angry outbursts, which are seldom as justified as his was. And if a stalwart champion of the

Lord like David could succumb both to adultery with Bathsheba and to the conspiratorial murder of her husband Uriah, we "ordinary" mortals need to beware the stress of temptation. Paul articulated the idea of mercy-activated insight: "[I]f you think you are standing, watch out that you do not fall" (1 Corinthians 10:12).

The Lord's "trick" of using failure to foster good makes the Portuguese proverb meaningful: "God draws straight with a crooked pen." By many such subtle "mercy interventions" God prevents the weeds of self-deception from strangling grace within our souls. This very prevention of discouragement is a seldom appreciated dimension of God's loving mercy—part of his "spiritual vaccination program."

One of God's most effective stratagems against discouragement (which is the favorite firearm of hell) is the force of the example of others around us—and of those who have gone before us, the saints who have left legacies of heroic virtue after slipping free of the bondages of sin. Peter, the first pope, denied Christ three times but is now a luminary of heaven. Paul was a full-fledged terrorist who relentlessly sought the imprisonment and death of Christians, even trying to persuade them to blaspheme God, but he went on to write thirteen Spirit-inspired epistles of the New Testament. Countless martyrs were garden-variety sinners who shed their blood for the King of Martyrs. Literally millions of God's children through the ages have, by their converted lives, chronicled the availability of his boundless mercy.

It was this consideration that led me one time, in a moment of levity, to dash off the following ditty:

> Peter thrice denied the Lord; Zacchaeus was a cheat;
> And then there was the prostitute who wept at
>   Jesus' feet.
> Simon was an anarchist; Mathew plundered taxes.
> The "sons of thunder," James and John, were angry
>   battle-axes,
> Like Paul, the rabid terrorist; and Dismas was a thief;
> Magdalene was demon-filled, and Thomas lacked belief.
> But there they are in heaven, smiling down upon
>   us now;
> Each wears a brilliant halo tilted on a battered brow.
> So things for us are looking up in this salvation
>   business—
> No matter what our "was-ness" was,
> What truly counts is "is-ness."

God's merciful love forever stands as an insuperable armamentarium. There is not one temptation or trial that can outstrip that divine power of compassionate mercy. Somehow it's consoling to know that Jesus began his ministry by shepherding a ragtag flock of black sheep to work with him.

"[My] power," the Lord revealed to Paul, "is made perfect in weakness." To which Paul responded:

> I will boast all the more gladly of my weaknesses, so that the power of Christ may dwell in me. Therefore I am content with weaknesses, insults, hardships, persecutions, and calamities for the sake of Christ; for whenever I am weak, then I am strong. (2 Corinthians 12:9–10)

In that paradox he saw the source of power of many Old Testament heroes whose weaknesses were turned into strengths (see Hebrews 11).

When we are discouraged and overwhelmed by our own spiritual weakness and ineptitude, it's consoling to remember that God isn't discouraged with us. It is then, recalling this often-forgotten aspect of his great mercy, that we should boast with holy boldness, "I can do all things through him who strengthens me" (Philippians 4:13). Divine Mercy even articulates in the Scriptures the how-to program for implementing this scenario: "Commit your work to the LORD, and your plans will be established" (Proverbs 16:3), and "In all your ways acknowledge him, and he will make straight your paths" (3:6).

There are many other avenues of grace—rivulets of God's love—that are enjoyed by souls who keep themselves enveloped in God's mercy. He graciously bestows his graces, and continuously too, since Jesus' intercession for us in heaven is continuous (Hebrews 7:25). Most of these graces will never be recognized or appreciated this side of heaven. In the endless ecstasy of love that awaits us, we will look back in astonished retrospect to appreciate this present beneficence.

THIRTEEN

CHANNELING GOD'S COMPASSION TO OTHERS

A little goes a long way for some things. It takes only microscopic portions of trace minerals such as phosphorus or magnesium to maintain cardiovascular health. Typical spider silk, of which cobwebs are composed, is stronger than steel of the same thickness; yet a single strand of this webbing, if it were long enough to stretch all the way around the world, would weigh less than a pound.

A little virtue in a God-focused person goes a long way too. The Creator's marvelous plan is to use his human creatures as the privileged instruments of the proliferation of his Divine Mercy to all of his precious people. "God is able to provide you with every blessing in abundance, so that by always having enough of everything, you may share abundantly in every good work" (2 Corinthians 9:8). Such "good works," when directed to the aid of our fellow humans in need, are called "works of mercy." Through Saint Faustina Jesus gave directions for

us to perform these works of mercy out of love for him—
"always and everywhere"—in three ways: by deed, by
word and by prayer.[1]

The *Catechism* reviews the traditional listing of the
"works of mercy" that we are called to perform:

> The *works of mercy* are charitable actions by which we
> come to the aid of our neighbor in his spiritual and bodily
> necessities. Instructing, advising, consoling, comforting
> are spiritual works of mercy, as are forgiving and bearing
> wrongs patiently. The corporal works of mercy consist
> especially in feeding the hungry, sheltering the homeless,
> clothing the naked, visiting the sick and imprisoned, and
> burying the dead. Among all these, giving alms to the
> poor is one of the chief witnesses to fraternal charity: it is
> also a work of justice pleasing to God. (#2447)

"[H]appy are those who are kind to the poor" (Proverbs
14:21).

The works of mercy are simply ways in which we
receive the vertically presented mercy of God and allow it
to be "horizontalized" through us. We become more and
more open channels of that mercy to others, fostering
within ourselves the loving concern of God for his people.
As parents in the procreation of their offspring are privileged to become participators in the creative power of the
Almighty, and as a priest becomes an instrument in the
flow of grace from God through his priesthood, derived
from Jesus, the Eternal Priest, so also anyone and everyone should enjoy the privilege of propagating mercy as
human instruments of the divine. Shakespeare expressed

it in these words: "We do pray for mercy; And that same prayer doth teach us all to render the deeds of mercy."[2]

Our God is a God of the hundredfold, whose return to us far exceeds the little we give him. He promises that "[a] good measure, pressed down, shaken together, running over, will be put into your lap" (Luke 6:38). Paul reminds us that the Lord "by the power at work within us is able to accomplish abundantly far more than all we can ask or imagine" (Ephesians 3:20).

A simple interior act of love directed to the hidden Christ-presence in a person whom you find hard to love, an interior act of humility when unthanked or falsely accused, a tiny effort to be patient with others or a love-motivated act of courtesy will cause the Lord to tug you close to his heart and grace-kiss your soul. As the old hair cream commercial put it, "A li'l dab'll do ya!"

Saint Thérèse of Lisieux's spirituality encompassed the same principle that Mother Teresa of Calcutta espoused: it isn't the greatness of the work that counts in God's eyes; it's the love with which it is undertaken. Love is the magnifier of all non-sinful activity, and the reward that it reaps is proportionate to the loving mercy or compassion that motivates it.

To get some idea of how the Lord likes to see his own mercy "teleported" to his people through each of us, we can recall the words of Jesus:

> Abide in me as I abide in you. Just as the branch cannot bear fruit by itself unless it abides in the vine, neither can you unless you abide in me. I am the vine, you are the branches. *Those who abide in me and I in them bear*

much fruit, because apart from me you can do nothing.
(John 15:4–5, italics mine)

So we strive to be merciful as our heavenly Father is merciful, as was Jesus himself.

The deeper we are immersed in the ambience of Jesus' own love, the more our works of mercy will bear fruit. Some of this fruit you will be allowed to see in this life, and you will be thrilled to know how the Lord has used you. But much of the fruit will be recognized only when you receive your eternal "paycheck" with its bonus.

If you need assurance of that bonus, read the encouraging words of Hebrews 6:10–12:

God is not unjust; he will not overlook your work and the love that you showed for his sake in serving the saints [the faithful], as you still do. And we want each one of you to show the same diligence so as to realize the full assurance of hope to the very end, so that you may not become sluggish, but imitators of those who through faith and patience inherit the promises.

One of the many unappreciated ways in which God exercises his compassionate mercy involves ever ubiquitous human suffering and adversity. "The LORD is near to the brokenhearted, and saves the crushed in spirit. Many are the afflictions of the righteous, but the LORD rescues them from them all" (Psalm 34:18–19). But he likes to accomplish this "rescue" through us humans as his privileged instruments. And very often he will choose those who have been severely tested and survived, because they are usually the best equipped to help their besieged brethren.

As a movement, Alcoholics Anonymous has found its greatest success in helping the addicted through the ministering of those who have struggled up the mountain of rehabilitation themselves; their empathy is almost miraculously therapeutic for other victims of addiction. That's the real fruit of their labors. Those who most closely abide as branches in the divine vine are the ones who will be most fruitful in their heroic efforts.

The best drill sergeant is not the deskbound general but the soldier who has served in the front lines of battle. Paul shows how God marshals our difficult experiences to teach us how to comfort others who lie wounded:

> [T]he God of all consolation...consoles us in all our affliction, so that we may be able to console those who are in any affliction with the consolation with which we ourselves are consoled by God. For just as the sufferings of Christ are abundant for us, so also our consolation is abundant through Christ. (2 Corinthians 1:3–5)

There is an eschatological dimension of that altruistic consolation—the reward element promised by Jesus: "Blessed are the merciful, for they will receive mercy" (Matthew 5:7). That refers primarily to God's merciful act of cleansing the compassionate and merciful person ("everything will be clean for you"—Luke 11:41), while increasing that person's merits (eternal reward). But also, centuries of Christian tradition and experience as well as Scripture have shown the reward to include even in this earthly life countless special blessings for the merciful and compassionate soul. "[I]f you offer your food to the hungry and satisfy the needs of the afflicted, then your light shall rise in the darkness and your gloom be like the noonday" (Isaiah 58:10–11).

No one can help the torn and anguished person more gently and sympathetically than one who remembers his or her own experience of pain or struggle. As Samuel Taylor Coleridge phrased it, "Pity is best taught by fellowship in woe."[3] The greatest champions of freedom are those who spent years in dank and filthy cells, tortured daily while languishing near starvation. As prisoners of those who sneered at human freedom, they came to appreciate the freedom for which they yearned. When tormented by malevolent demons whose cruel plans for us include affliction or inducements to evil, a word of encouragement from another who has survived such adversities is like cool water to a parched desert straggler.

The mandate of Jesus is broad enough to encompass every possible trial and tribulation: "Be merciful, just as your Father is merciful" (Luke 6:36). Spiritual "survivors" are called to be agents of God in supporting those undergoing similar distress. Jean Jacques Rousseau may have overstated this point, but his observation smacks of truth: "We pity in others only those evils that we have ourselves experienced."[4]

By such support a languishing soul can come to realize that its transitory trials and temptations are to be used as plantings toward a harvest with permanent reward and comfort. These experiences of life, more than tutors or book knowledge, enable us to convey to the brokenhearted the consolation and conviction of God's love.

Horace Mann, in his *Lectures on Education*, said, "To pity distress is but human; to relieve it is Godlike."[5]

It is not just the trial-tested who are called to encourage others; Jesus himself takes on that task also. The same Jesus who applied to himself Isaiah's prophecy about coming to "bind up the brokenhearted to proclaim liberty to the captives, and release to the prisoners [of sin]" (Isaiah 61:1, as quoted by Jesus in Luke 4:18) suffered affliction and temptation himself.

One outstanding function of the Lord's compassionate mercy is his assistance in a special area among the many types of healing—that of the ever-growing problem of spiritual warfare. He is always ready to support us in our struggle against the fiendish plots of the enemy.

The Christian who has felt the iron rule of Satan knows how to escape. He runs to the Word of God and lays open his heart to Christ, knowing that "the Son of God was revealed for this purpose, to destroy the works of the devil" (1 John 3:8). Jesus said, "[T]he ruler of this world…has no power over me" (John 14:30).

Jesus demonstrated his compassionate mercy in his personal prayer to suppress the attacks of the powers of hell: "Satan has demanded to sift all of you like wheat, but I have prayed for you that your…faith may not fail" (Luke 22:31–32). In teaching his disciples to be merciful as their heavenly Father is merciful in their mission of deliverance, Jesus added the mandate to extend that God-given freedom to others: "[W]hen once you have turned back, strengthen your brothers" (Luke 22:32).

Coming close to temptation or trial from our arch-enemy can provide experience that prompts us to warn others about the draw of devilment and, in appropriate situations, to become instrumental in their deliverance: "[S]igns will accompany those who believe: by using my name they will cast out demons" (Mark 16:17). Even after his ascension into heaven, "the Lord worked with [the apostles] and confirmed the message by...signs" (verse 20). He continues to support his people today with his mercy.

FOURTEEN

WHY ARE YOU CARRYING THAT ANVIL?

A slightly built man applied for a job as a stevedore, which required hand-loading heavy items to docked ships. The supervisor was hesitant to hire him because of his apparently frail physique, but he decided to let him try.

The first day the little man was struggling alone to load a 150-pound anvil when he tripped and fell off the gangplank into deep water. He immediately called for someone to throw him a rope and pull him to safety. After repeated calls for help with no response, he finally threatened, "If someone doesn't throw me a rope soon, I'm going to drop this anvil!"

That tale elicits at least a chuckle from most people, but it depicts a truly serious situation in what many of us experience every day: that is, the heroic struggle to sustain onerous burdens that seem overwhelming to us, with apparently no help available, even from the Lord. If providential design seems to cause or permit our life's burdens, then Jesus' hint of help may sound almost like mockery: "My yoke is easy and my burden is light" (Matthew 11:30).

When oppressed with problems, hardships and troubles on every side, it isn't difficult to identify with David in his depression:

> I cry aloud to God,
>> aloud to God, that he may hear me.
> In the day of my trouble I seek the Lord;
>> in the night my hand is stretched out without wearying;
>> my soul refuses to be comforted.
> I think of God, and I moan;
>> I meditate, and my spirit faints. (Psalm 77:1–3)

We try to solve our problems by every means at our disposal. "God helps those who help themselves," we figure. Then, when we exhaust our own means, we look to the standard advice: "If all else fails, follow directions." And where better to look for directions than in that timeless direction-book called the Bible.

TAKE UP YOUR CROSS

The first thing you will learn from the direction-book is that suffering in itself is simply distress, while suffering with love is a cross. (If it is task-related, it might be called a yoke.) The bottom line is your ability to grasp the full implication of what a cross really is and what it is designed to do for you. That itself is a grace from God.

A typical commercial plane can carry about 1.3 times its own weight in passengers and luggage. Aerodynamically speaking, a dragonfly is superior: It can easily flight-lift seven times its own weight. But when the burdens of life weigh us humans down, we find that we just don't fly. From the time of Christ, people have given a name to these burdens: they're called crosses.

Even before Jesus carried and died on his own cross, he told his disciples, "If any want to become my followers, let them deny themselves and take up their cross daily and follow me" (Luke 9:23). In citing that classic passage, we often overlook the word "daily." For most persons it is not too hard to put up with even a heavy burden for a short while. But on our long "transcontinental" flight from here to eternity, long-term hardships—that is, the daily, ongoing troubles—can be truly wearisome. It's not the sword thrust of martyrdom that's hard; it's the persistent, frequent, daily pinpricks.

Yet the weight of our burdens seems to decrease as our strength increases with daily, love-charged perseverance. Every burden-wearied person can find strength-restoring rest in loving intimacy with Jesus. His words encompass one of the most touching but least acknowledged expressions of God's gentle loving mercy:

> Come to me, all you that are weary and are carrying heavy burdens, and I will give you rest. Take my yoke upon you, and learn from me; for I am gentle and humble in heart, and you will find rest for your souls. For my yoke is easy, and my burden is light. (Matthew 11:28–30)

We find this rest in Jesus *only* if we profoundly understand the first three words of the passage and put them into practice in a meaningful way: "Come to me." For only in that heart-to-heart union with the Lord can we receive the "rest" that he promises. The invitation is reiterated in Hebrews 4:16: "Let us therefore approach the throne of grace with boldness, so that we may receive mercy and find grace to help in time of need."

Among the common burdens that we humans bear, that of illness deserves a special word of explanation. There is no scriptural indication that sickness is part of "God's will" or an end in itself. But our Catholic faith recognizes the value of "redemptive" human suffering. All human suffering is extrinsic—that is, not intrinsically the cause of the divine act of redemption, although it may conjoin it. Yet suffering can be called "intrinsic" in that its cause is a force inside oneself. When properly embraced as God's will, it enjoys a "participatively redemptive" power that is derived from one's spiritual union with Christ in his redemptive suffering.

This is explained in several paradoxical "rejoice in suffering" passages. One is from Paul, Colossians 1:24: "I am now rejoicing in my sufferings for your sake, and in my flesh I am completing what is lacking in Christ's afflictions for the sake of his body, that is, the church." And Peter wrote in the same context of rejoicing in suffering, even embracing it with delight: "[R]ejoice insofar as you are sharing Christ's sufferings, so that you may also be glad and shout for joy when his glory is revealed" (1 Peter 4:13). This is a delight not in the hardship of suffering but in being incorporated into the divine dynamic of the great redemptive act of God toward his infected but deeply loved human race.

Archbishop Sheen once poetized the concept with the

remark that by such "co-redemptive" suffering anyone can be said to be "a redeemer with a small *r*." Any person who is gifted with this ability to rejoice in sufferings because of being redemptively united with the Redeemer is a person who sees the unavoidable sufferings as camouflaged treasures of God's mercy.

An analogy may help to understand how one can rejoice in suffering although not because of it. Consider the patient who eagerly submits to surgery though knowing that it will be painful. The person can be happy about the medical procedure because it will provide healing ultimately. Such a person realizes the tremendous advantage of having a skilled surgeon available when the vast majority of humans lack even basic medical care.

Similarly, the spiritually mature person sees hardship not as mere pain but as love-clothed pain. The pain is a cross but also a paradoxical unfolding of the Lord's mercy—his merciful love. Embracing God-sent or God-allowed suffering with a surrendering love releases floods of grace on such a soul as well as inestimable heavenly rewards or merits. The Divine Mercy aspect of the situation is the person's awareness that "*in the Lord* your labor is not in vain," as Paul reminds us in 1 Corinthians 15:58.

But "extrinsic" suffering, whether caused by the malice of others (persecution, social injustice, an unloving spouse and so forth) or by nonmalicious means (such as weather inclemency or accidents), are situations that express God's *permissive* will. Jesus' counsel to "take up your cross and follow me" refers mainly to this extrinsic suffering. He himself was victimized in being condemned and tortured to death on Calvary. On the other hand, it is safe to assume that God usually wants us to be healed of sickness (a type of intrinsic suffering). Much has been written on this subject in charismatic healing literature, expounding the so-called "fourth century theology of suffering."

It seems that Jesus' suffering during his earthly life was entirely an "extrinsic" form of suffering. He certainly experienced the normal discomforts of hunger, fatigue, heat and cold and so on, but free as he was from the contamination of original sin, he probably never experienced illness in his perfectly healthy body. Yet he suffered far more than almost any one of us has ever suffered. In this sense he was like us; "we do not have a high priest who is unable to sympathize with our weaknesses" (Hebrews 4:15).

GOD'S WILL AND HIS MERCY

But was it "according to God's will"—the will of his heavenly Father—that Jesus should suffer? Why would any loving father want his beloved son to suffer?

By the same token we might ask, does God really want us to suffer? Does he gloat over our sufferings as if they provide some form of divine fulfillment? Does our suffering really fulfill God's will and thus make him happy?

Jeremiah gives the incisive answer to that question: "Although he causes grief, he will have compassion [mercy] according to the abundance of his steadfast love; for he does not willingly afflict or grieve anyone" (Lamentations 3:31–33). That is, God doesn't "gloat" over anyone's suffering, no matter how small or great it may be.

In response to questions about how our suffering can fulfill God's will, the bottom line is that God sometimes wills our suffering *permissively* and sometimes *positively*. The latter type is his discipline to turn sinners away from sin, as a father who loves his child will discipline that child for his or her own good. The exceptional suffering sent as discipline to convert sinners is not an act of vengeance on God's part but a carefully executed act of mercy! If you interiorly resist that important truth, then prayerfully consider what God's word says about this:

> [W]e had human parents to discipline us, and we respected them. Should we not be even more willing to be subject to the Father of spirits and live? For they disciplined us for a short time as seemed best to them, but he disciplines us for our good, in order that we may share his holiness. Now, discipline always seems painful rather than pleasant at the time, but later it yields the peaceful fruit of righteousness to those who have been trained by it. (Hebrews 12:9–11)

Remember that when God wills suffering, he wills it as a means, not as an end in itself. By analogy, you may *permissively* will to undergo the inconvenience and fatigue of travel in order to enjoy a vacation that you *positively* will or desire. God permissively willed Jesus' suffering for many reasons, some of which include his desire to show vividly the extent of redemptive love: "No one has greater love than this, to lay down one's life for one's friends" (John 15:13). He willed it as a repentance-eliciting action and as an example for us in patience, fortitude and forgiveness.

Likewise, as a function of his loving mercy, God *permissively* wills our suffering for many reasons, as God's word illustrates. Paul obviously pondered his own trials in this light: "We are afflicted in every way, but not crushed; *perplexed*, but not driven to despair" (2 Corinthians 4:8, italics mine).

God's mercy is not limited to *supporting* us in our afflictions; it often reaches far beyond that. He often provides *healing* of those very afflictions, particularly when several conditions are fulfilled, such as having "mountain-moving" faith. For more about this subject, see my book and tape album *When God Says No: 25 Reasons Why Some Prayers Aren't Answered*.[1]

FIFTEEN

GOD'S HIDING PLACE: AFFLICTION WITHOUT RESTRICTION

A wife inquired of her husband, "Why do you always answer my questions by asking another one?"

"Do I?" was the inevitable response.

Even God sometimes answers questions by asking other questions, as he did in response to Job's direct challenge: "Let the Almighty answer me" (Job 31:35). Job's was simply the most perplexing problem ever explored by human thinkers: the "why" of the suffering of the innocent.

The Lord's answer-by-way-of-question, "Who is this that darkens counsel by words without knowledge?" (Job 38:2; see also 42:3), provided for Job, in a staggering theophany, a mystical insight into the purpose and value of suffering. That very revelation, though not detailed in Scripture for us whose curiosity exceeds our blind trust in Providence, was nevertheless one of the greatest disclosures by the Almighty of what are known as the "positive" (grace-providing) aspects of his great attribute of mercy. These reach beyond the "negative" aspect of his mercy, the remission of sin and guilt. And interestingly, as part of the overall divine didactics, the Lord excoriated Job's three well-intentioned friends (see Job 42:7) who, like countless superficial thinkers through the ages, had presented wrong answers to the perennial question of seemingly undeserved and senseless suffering.

Without a prodigious outpouring of the Holy Spirit's gifts of wisdom, understanding and knowledge about God's will (see Colossians 1:9), we can't expect to enjoy the insight given to Job. But by employing rigorous theology we can explore both the cause (etiology) of suffering and its purpose (teleology). We find multiple rationales for God's will in suffering—whether it occurs by *his positive will* (leading to spiritual discipline and growth, purification, fortitude, patience, compassion and so on) or by his *permissive will* (allowing human malice or negligence to cause suffering in ourselves or in others, and even allowing Satan and his minions to cause us incalculable suffering).

Your cross may redound to good in some unexpected way (see Isaiah 38:17; Jeremiah 29:11; Romans 8:28; Philippians 1:19). In the history of God's purpose in suffering, Paul includes, among other things, "our inner nature …being renewed day by day" and, above all, an overwhelmingly disproportionate reward: "an eternal weight of glory beyond all measure" (see 2 Corinthians 4:16, 17). He reaffirms this latter benefit in Romans 8:18: "I consider that the sufferings of this present time are not worth comparing with the glory about to be revealed to us."

Peter too reminds us that ours is "an inheritance that is imperishable, undefiled, and unfading, kept in heaven," while even on Earth we "are being protected by the power of God through faith." So we can "rejoice, even if now for a little while [we] have had to suffer various trials" (see 1 Peter 1:4–6).

Meditating on all this gives the problem of suffering a more proper perspective, and embracing God's will in suffering becomes less difficult. With Jesus as our great exemplar in embracing God's will in suffering (see 1 Peter:1–2), our bitter trials become bittersweet, and they continue to grow sweeter as we hunger more and more for God's will and revel in his mercy even when it is mysteriously expressed in our suffering (see Proverbs 27:7). All of the many ways in which good comes from adversity can be occasions of a gushing outflow of Divine Mercy.

I discovered in one theological treatise a list of nineteen reasons or purposes for suffering, all derived from Scripture. The preponderant ones I have dealt with in some detail in my booklet and tape titled *Seven Answers to the "Why" of Suffering*.[1] This present brief review of the great problem of suffering primarily is intended to show how it is so beautifully incorporated into the dynamic of Divine Mercy. Saint Faustina, in her role of championing the teachings on God's mercy, learned those truths only in the Lord's best classroom—the crucible of suffering.

THREE SOURCES OF SUFFERING

We find the immediate causes of suffering in humans, in the devil and in God (yes, God!). Let's start with humans.

For our part suffering finds its origin in sin—starting with the original sin in the Garden of Eden. Furthermore, ancestral sin can bring suffering to offspring: "Our ancestors sinned; they are no more, and we bear their iniquities" (Lamentations 5:7). (See my book *Healing Your Family Tree*[2] for more details on this.) Finally, personal sin can bring its own suffering.

For instance, sins of sexual promiscuity, gluttony, drug abuse, drunkenness and the like can cause physical, emotional, social, financial and spiritual suffering to oneself and others. Paul starkly reminds us that even sins of sacrilegious Communion can cause illness and death (see 1 Corinthians 11:30). While guilt is often at the root of this type of suffering, even sinless infants can suffer from the sins of others, as did also Jesus and his sinless mother.

The second source of suffering is the devil. He not only stokes the fires of hell for the reprobate, as it were, but also, with inexpressible malevolence, assigns myriads of demons to cause anguish among us humans on Earth (see Ephesians 6:12). "Like a roaring lion your adversary the devil prowls around, looking for someone to devour" (1 Peter 5:8).

God can allow Satan to pursue even his holy ones. Twice God explicitly permitted Satan to harm Job (1:12 and 2:6) because of the foreseen good that would eventuate from those trials. Job was extremely holy, as God himself attested: "There is no one like him on the earth, a blameless and upright man who fears God and turns away from evil" (Job 1:8). Yet he suffered the loss of his vast wealth, his livestock, his health, even his house and his family in a tornado.

A spirit of depression was sent to torment King Saul (see 1 Samuel 16:14–15). Paul warned of dangers from an evil spirit of bondage (2 Corinthians 11:4), and he himself suffered physically from what he called "a thorn . . . in the flesh" caused by an evil spirit of infirmity, "a messenger of Satan" (12:7). These and other types of demons afflict countless people today. Very few of these anguished souls can find even a glimmer of God's loving mercy in the context of demon-permitted suffering. It took Job a long time to see God's mercy in such harrowing situations.

The devil and his demons don't cause all our suffering, but they certainly cause much of it. Jesus promised that "the ruler of this world will be driven out" (John 12:31). And the final relief from this suffering will be attained when Jesus' own suffering (verses 32–33) will be fully applied. In fact, "The Son of God was revealed [incarnationally] for this purpose, to destroy the works of the devil" (1 John 3:8).

Finally, let's look to God as a possible cause of suffering. This divine source itself has a triple purpose: First, God can cause suffering as a punishment, although punishment is always coactively induced by the victim's human malice: "Your ways and your doings have brought this upon you. This is your doom [punishment]" (Jeremiah 4:18; see also 1 Thessalonians 4:3–6). Keep in mind, as already explained, that punishment from God is an act of justice that is restorative, not vindictive.

Secondly, God can cause suffering as a corrective measure, as the author of Hebrews states: "Endure trials…as discipline…. [God] disciplines us for our good, in order that we may share his holiness…. [L]ater it yields the peaceful fruit of righteousness to those who have been trained by it" (Hebrews 12:7; 10–11). Read that Scripture again, carefully!

Thirdly, in affliction God disciplines us as a perfecting process—again, never gloatingly or vengefully. Like a parent submitting a child to painful surgery, he acts with love, not anger. "Although he causes grief, he will have compassion according to the abundance of his steadfast love; for he does not willingly afflict or grieve anyone" (Lamentations 3:32–33).

Here we see another manifestation of Divine Providence, the unfolding of God's wisdom and knowledge and goodness. His loving mercy ever engineers an inscrutable but marvelous and gracious design. "I know the plans I have for you, says the LORD, plans for your welfare and not for harm, to give you a future with hope" (Jeremiah 29:11).

ALL THINGS WORK FOR GOOD

At this juncture the causes of suffering begin to reflect their sublime purpose, which is ultimately good, not bad. Paul's indomitable Christian optimism blazed beyond his prison cell when he wrote, while still shackled, his poignant words to the Philippians: "I will continue to rejoice, for I know that through your prayers and the help of the Spirit of Jesus Christ this will turn out for my deliverance" (1:18–19).

For anyone asking the why of innocent suffering, God's word reiterates that the end result will be for one's good, as it was for Job. Whatever the suffering—from a hangnail to a holocaust, from torture to a tornado—"*all things* work together for the good of those who love [God], who are called according to his purpose [his will]" (Romans 8:28, italics mine). If suffering is truly for the good of those who love him, it is clearly one of the positive aspects of his mercy—providing good for us even from hurtful events in our lives.

Are we really willing to be "trained" by suffering or, for that matter, trained by any other rigorous spiritual formation? Paul was clearly trained by his false accusations and imprisonment, among other forms of suffering:

> I have learned to be content with whatever I have. I know what it is to have little, and I know what it is to have plenty. In any and all circumstances I have learned the secret of being well-fed and of going hungry, of having plenty and of being in need. I can do all things through him who strengthens me. (Philippians 4:11–13)

Paul saw too benefits beyond that of his own holiness:

> I want you to know, beloved, that what has happened to me has actually helped to spread the gospel, so that it has become known throughout the whole imperial guard and to everyone else that my imprisonment is for Christ; and most of the brothers and sisters, having been made confident in the Lord by my imprisonment, dare to speak the word with greater boldness and without fear. (Philippians 1:12–14)

This kind of response is rare among God's people, even out of the question for most of the faltering sheep in the flock of the Good Shepherd. The exceptions are those precious souls who, like the magnanimous apostle Paul, have allowed themselves to be open to God's grace. Indoing so they have learned that God's mercy is his answer to our misery.

To be "trained" by affliction is to find it always easy to surrender to the enfolding open arms and nail-pierced hands of our compassionate Savior. It is to have mastered the loving response to God's welcome in whatever circumstances his love permits. It is to incorporate into one's life a deeper meaning of the word *heartfelt*—namely, "taking to heart" the exciting revelations from our beloved Savior about the *awesome mercy of God*.

NOTES

CHAPTER ONE: A Heaven-Designed Jigsaw Puzzle

1. Saint Augustine, *Commentary on the Gospel of John*, Tractate 12, 13, in J.P. Migne, *Patrologia Latina* (Paris, 1841–1855), quoted in *Catechism of the Catholic Church*, (Washington: United States Catholic Conference; Libreria Editrice Vaticana, 1997), #1458.

2. Council of Trent (1547), Denzinger-Schonmetzer, *Enchiridion Symbolorum, definitionum et declarationum de rebus fidei et morum* (1965), 1528, quoted in CCC, #1989.

3. Henry Ward Beecher, quoted at yah2004.tripod.com.

4. See www.quote-fox.com: "If God created us in his own image, we have more than reciprocated."

5. C.S. Lewis, *The Problem of Pain*, quoted at en.thinkexist.com.

6. Sister M. Faustina Kowalska, *Diary of Sister M. Faustina Kowalska: Divine Mercy in My Soul*, 3rd ed. with revisions (Stockbridge, Mass.: Marian, 2004), p. 699.

CHAPTER THREE: God's Poor Memory

1. Clifton Fadiman, ed., *The Little, Brown Book of Anecdotes* (Boston: Little, Brown, & Co., 1985), p. 140.

2. Abraham Lincoln, in William Barclay, *The Gospel of Luke* (Louisville, Ky.: Knox, 2001), p. 244.

3. William Shakespeare, "The Merchant of Venice," Act IV, Scene 1, in *The Portable Shakespeare* (New York: Penguin, 1972), p. 627.

4. Saint Augustine, quoted at www.brainyquote.com.

CHAPTER FOUR: Repentance: The Soul's "Delete" Function

1. "The Merchant of Venice," Act IV, scene 1.

2. Saint Thomas Aquinas, *Summa Theologica*, I, q. 21, art. 4, in *St. Thomas and the Summa Theologica* software (Gervais, Ore.: Harmony, 1998).

CHAPTER FIVE: Roadblocks to Mercy: Counterfeit Repentance

1. Voltaire, quoted at www.brainyquote.com.

2. Oprah Winfrey, quoted at tkdtutor.com.

CHAPTER SIX: Seven Misunderstandings About Repentance

1. Alexander Pope quoting Homer, *Iliad*, Book XV, 1, 227, as cited in *12,000 Religious Quotations* (Grand Rapids, Mich.: Baker, 1989), p. 376.

2. Walter Hilton, *The Scale of Perfection*, quoted at www.martinisrael.u-net.com.

3. Thomas Carlyle, quoted in *12,000 Religious Quotations*, p. 406.

4. Martin Luther, quoted in *12,000 Religious Quotations*, p. 377.

5. Saint Francis de Sales, quoted in Jill Haak Adule, *The Wisdom of the Saints* (New York: Oxford University Press, 1987), p. 148.

6. Saint Augustine, Sermon 3.

7. Henry Ward Beecher, first part quoted in *Your Ultimate Success Quotation Library* downloadable software; second part quoted at www.quotationspage.com.

8. Saint Augustine, quoted in *12,000 Religious Quotations*, p. 275.

CHAPTER EIGHT: Go to Hell—But Only If You Choose to Go

1. Fadiman, p. 140.

2. See Pope John Paul II, *Dives in Misericordia*, "On the Mercy of God," November 30, 1980.

3. Charles Sprague, quoted in *The New Dictionary of Thought* (Garden City, N.Y.: Hanover, 1960), p. 405, and in *12,000 Religious Quotations*, p. 302.

4. *Summa*, I, q. 21, art. 3.

CHAPTER TEN: Mercy in Cosmic Camouflage: Providence at Work

1. *Summa*, I, q. 20, art. 4.

2. Voltaire, quoted at wikipedia.org.

3. *Diary*, p. 1578.

CHAPTER ELEVEN: God Thinks Big—He Made Elephants, Didn't He?

1. Saint Augustine, *Confessions*, quoted in *12,000 Religious Quotations*, p. 301.

2. Saint Augustine, quoted in *12,000 Religious Quotations*, p. 375.

3. Jeremy Taylor, quoted in *12,000 Religious Quotations*, p. 302.

CHAPTER TWELVE: Divine Mercy as a Sin Vaccine

1. *Summa*, II-I, q. 111, art. 3.

2. *Diary*, p. 422.

CHAPTER THIRTEEN: Channeling God's Compassion to Others

1. *Diary*, p. 742.

2. *The Merchant of Venice*, Act IV, scene 1.

3. Samuel Taylor Coleridge, quoted in *12,000 Religious Quotations*, p. 330.

4. Jean Jacques Rousseau, quoted in *12,000 Religious Quotations*, p. 330.

5. Horace Mann, *Lectures on Education*, Lecture VI (1845), quoted in *12,000 Religious Quotations*, p. 330.

CHAPTER FOURTEEN: Why Are You Carrying That Anvil?

1. John H. Hampsch, *When God Says No: 25 Reasons Why Some Prayers Aren't Answered* (Huntington, Ind.: Our Sunday Visitor, 1994).

CHAPTER FIFTEEN: God's Hiding Place: Affliction Without Restriction

1. John H. Hampsch, *Seven Answers to the "Why" of Suffering* (Santa Barbara Calif.: Queenship Publishing Co., 2000).

2. John H. Hampsch, *Healing Your Family Tree* (Santa Barbara, Calif.: Queenship Publishing Co., 1999).